738.12   167931
Woo   Wood, Nigel

                Oriental glazes

DATE DUE

CERAMIC SKILLBOOKS

Series Editor:
Murray Fieldhouse

Oriental Glazes

Their Chemistry, Origins and Re-creation

Nigel Wood

PITMAN/WATSON GUPTILL

PITMAN PUBLISHING LIMITED
39 Parker Street, London WC2B 5PB

Associated Companies

Copp Clark Limited, Toronto
Pitman Publishing Co. SA (Pty) Ltd, Johannesburg
Pitman Publishing New Zealand Ltd, Wellington
Pitman Publishing Pty Ltd, Melbourne

First published by Pitman Publishing Ltd 1978
Published in the USA by Watson-Guptill 1978

© Pitman Publishing 1978

WATSON-GUPTILL PUBLICATIONS
a division of Billboard Publications Inc.,
1515 Broadway, New York, N.Y. 10036

UK ISBN 0 273 01102 2 (cased edition)
UK ISBN 0 273 01056 5 (paperback edition)
US ISBN 0-8230-3385-6

Text set in 10/11 pt IBM Century, printed by photolithography, and bound in
Great Britain at The Pitman Press, Bath

167931

Contents

Introduction

High-fired glazes were first made in China about three-and-a-half thousand years ago, reached their greatest quality over seven hundred years ago, and are still in production today. Western stoneware and porcelain glazes, by comparison, have barely begun their history and the possibilities of learning from China's thousands of years of experience with high-fired pottery are still largely unexplored. This book is an attempt to bring together as much as possible of the technical information that has been accumulating over the years on the subject. This information enables us to compare numerous analyses of China's finest glazes and, thanks to the arrival of cheap electronic calculators, to re-create some of these glazes for use on our own pottery.

Admittedly there are still some large gaps in our understanding of Far Eastern glazes — the two most obvious being that we know very little about Korean glazes (other than what we can guess), and the magnificent dark iron-glazes of Sung China, known by the Japanese name *temmoku* have received nothing like the attention that Chinese celadons, for example, have enjoyed. Both Korean glazes and Chinese temmokus have to be studied by the less satisfactory method of comparing them with glazes that we do know something about, and hoping that the analyses will eventually appear that will settle the matter one way or another. Siamese glazes too are rather poorly documented, but ancient and modern Japanese glazes have had a good deal written about them — and the Japanese have also produced some very interesting work of their own on early Chinese glazes.

Probably the most important technical work on classic Chinese glazes will prove to be that now being carried out in China at the ceramic research institutes in Shanghai and Ching-tê Chên, where many of the old glazes are being re-created and a certain amount of this work has been included in this book. Fortunately, the more material that is compared, the clearer the subject becomes. The finest clays and glazes used in China embody certain essential principles of chemical construction that have been adhered to for hundreds of years and it is the demonstration and subsequent use of these principles that is the main point of this book.

Fig. 1 Honan temmoku jar with iron painting (height 8·5 inches). *Victoria and Albert Museum*

4

Fig. 2 Stoneware jar with 'bronze-type' lugs (height 13·5 inches). 1st century B.C. to 1st century A.D. 'Proto-porcelain' or 'Proto-Yüeh' ware and probably from North Chekiang. This hard, dark-firing stoneware was made from a siliceous clay rich in alkalis and iron, and the glaze is of a type that could have been made from a mixture of the body clay with lime (or limestone) in roughly 2:1 proportions. Rather less iron-rich clays of a similar type were used for the later Yüeh and celadon wares of Chekiang province. The parallel ridges are practical as well as decorative.
Victoria and Albert Museum

1 China's Early Lime Glazes

Some idea of the enormous lead that China holds with its experience of high-fired glazes comes from realizing that glazed stoneware was first made during China's bronze age — the Shang dynasty — and dates from about 1500 B.C. Nearly two thousand years were to pass before similar glazes began to appear in Korea and Japan, and another thousand before they were made in the West. By the time low-fired glazes came to be used on Chinese pottery the high-fired stoneware tradition was already over a thousand years old.

It is still something of a mystery exactly what materials the Chinese used to make these first high-fired glazes. It may be that the powerful fluxing effect of white-hot wood ash in the flames of the furnace produced a reaction with the surfaces of the pots to make the glazes, but the glazes seem rather too even for this to have definitely been the case. It is possible that the half a dozen known examples of Shang glazed stoneware represent a second stage in glaze development where the accidental glazing by ash during the firing has already been superseded by the deliberate application of ash (or ash-slag) to the pots before they were set in the kiln.

Felspathic and lime glazes

For some reason early Chinese glazes have come to be known as 'felspathic', suggesting that the bulk of the glaze recipe was provided by felspar. In fact felspar is by no means an indispensable material for high-fired glazes, and true felspathic glazes are actually rather rare in Chinese ceramics, though quite common in Japan. But both by analysis and appearance, it can be seen that early Chinese glazes belong to the other great family of stoneware glazes known as 'calcareous' or 'lime' glazes. These glazes are fluxed with lime in the form of wood ash, or crushed or burnt limestone.

The basic chemistry of lime glazes is fairly simple and good stoneware glazes of this type can be made with only three oxides: lime (calcium oxide), silica (silicon dioxide) and alumina (aluminium oxide). Individually these three oxides are some of the most un-meltable substances known, but in the correct proportions they will combine to give good stoneware glazes at about 1200°C.[1]†

Most of the early Chinese stoneware glazes are probably not too unlike the kind of glaze that can be made by mixing equal parts of pure clay, quartz and lime,* although this is merely *one* approach to providing the ultimate analysis that represents its true nature, and it is likely that many different recipes have been used in China to make this type of glaze. The natural impurities found in the ordinary clays, ashes and limestones used in the different recipes affect the colours and fluidity of these glazes, but they still show a strong 'family likeness' which is, technically, the result of their being low in silica and high in lime. The clay-quartz-lime glaze, which is actually the lowest-melting combination of the three oxides, silica, alumina and lime, is known as an 'eutectic mixture' and has the following ultimate analysis:

	Silica	*Alumina*	*Lime*
Silica-alumina-lime eutectic:	SiO_2	Al_2O_3	CaO
(per cent by weight)[2]	62·0	14·75	23·5

This eutectic mixture melts at 1170°C and makes a satisfactory glaze at about 1200°C. It probably formed the 'backbone' of most early Chinese stoneware glazes because its particular oxide balance could readily be achieved with so many common raw-materials — particularly with mixtures of clay and ash.

Clay and ash glazes

Lime is the major flux in most wood ashes, while silica and alumina are the main oxides in clays. Good lime glazes can, therefore, be made simply by adding ashes to clays — the quality of the glazes produced depending on the proportions used, and the silica and flux contents of the clays and ashes.

Because they share the same basic chemistry, glazes made from clay and ash and those made from clay, quartz and limestone can look very similar, and the strong links between them can be demonstrated as follows:

Ideal lime glaze: *pure clay + silica + calcium carbonate*
Clay and ash glaze: (*impure clay*) + (*ordinary wood ash*)

In the second recipe roughly equal parts of clay and ash have been used to make a glaze. About half the silica needed for the 'ideal' glaze has been provided by the impure (ordinary) clay, and all the lime and the remaining silica by the wood ash.

†Numbers in brackets indicate bibliography references, pages 92—94.
* The theoretical recipe is: kaolin 30.4, calcite 33.6 and quartz 36 — but as most china clays contain a small percentage of quartz, the 'equal parts' recipe is just as accurate.

The commonest fault with glazes made from mixtures of ordinary clay and ash (from the technical, rather than the aesthetic point of view) is that they tend to be too low in silica — the combined silica from the two materials being not quite enough to achieve the 'ideal' glaze, with the result that the glazes tend to run badly if overfired. This limits the potential for developing this kind of glaze. There is, however, another typically Chinese approach to glaze-making where limestone, or slaked lime, is mixed with *highly siliceous* clays, and this gives stoneware glazes with much greater potential for improvement.

Chinese glazes made from clay and lime

This recipe produces an essentially South Chinese type of glaze for it relies on the kind of high-silica, high-alkali clays found south of the Yangtse river (particularly in Chekiang province) but hardly at all in North China. It has been suggested that glazes made from mixtures of these siliceous clays with limestone or slaked lime were used for early Southern stonewares[3] (see Fig. 2). The logic behind this type of glaze (still used today in South China) can be seen by comparing it with the 'ideal' lime glaze — as was previously done with the clay and ash glaze:

Ideal lime glaze: *pure clay + silica + calcium carbonate*
Siliceous clay mixed with
limestone or slaked-lime: *(natural high-silica clay)* + *(limestone or lime)*

The difference between this recipe and the clay and ash glaze is that in this case all the silica is provided by the naturally siliceous clay, and all the calcium by limestone or slaked lime. This is the type of recipe that was probably used on the Southern stonewares of the Han and Six Dynasties eras (known as 'proto-porcelain') and analysis suggests that the proportions of clay to lime in these glazes may have been about two parts clay to one part limestone or lime.

Yet another approach to making this type of lime glaze is used in present day Chunking, in south-western China, where the country potters use a mixture of slaked lime, rice-husk ash, and clay to make their stoneware glazes. Rice-husk ash is almost pure silica and replaces quartz in the ideal recipe. The similarity of this recipe used by the Chunking potters, to the $1170°$ lime eutectic can be seen when the two glazes are compared:

	SiO_2	Al_2O_3	CaO	MgO	Fe_2O_3
$1170°$ Silica—alumina—lime eutectic:	62·0	14·75	23·25		
Chunking country pottery glaze (modern):[4]	62·7	13·8	20·5	1·5	1·3

Not only do clay and ash, and clay and lime glazes make good chemical sense, they also solve the practical problem of applying the glaze to the raw pot and making it stay there as the pot shrinks, expands, and then shrinks again during the processes of drying and firing — the clay in the glaze 'keeps step' with the clay of the pot.

The character of lime glazes

The earliest Chinese glazes were usually either glassy or somewhat dull, and these are typical characteristics of glazes high in calcium oxide. The dullness is caused by the large amounts of lime in the glazes having crystallized slightly in the cooling to give a dull, slightly papery appearance to the semi-transparent glazes.

Another, and more dramatic, type of high-lime glaze is produced when the molten glaze forms a complex pattern of streaks and wandering rivulets of thick glaze on a thinner background. Sometimes this spontaneous patterning is on a large scale, but it can also appear as a simple, overall mottling reminiscent of saltglaze. This effect occurs in glazes that are particularly high in lime and low in silica. These glazes are often unstable and where this natural patterning appears, the pots are often made with raised or deeply incised lines around them, to arrest the flowing glaze.

When the 'dull' type of glaze has been fired to a higher temperature, all the lime in the glaze takes part in the reaction to dissolve the silica and produces a glaze with a plain, watery, 'straightforward' glassiness. There is a narrow temperature range between the temperatures which produce the glassiness and the dullness where a lime glaze shows the softness and depth typical of celadons. Unfortunately this range was too narrow to be useful in most lime glazes, and Chinese potters had to progress to the more sophisticated lime-alkali glazes before they could exploit this quality properly.

From lime to lime-alkali glazes

The lime-alkali glazes of the Sung dynasties (A.D. 960—1279), typified by Chüns and celadons, are some of the finest stoneware glazes ever made, being equalled only by some Korean celadons, probably of a similar type. Between these glazes and the lime glazes so far discussed is a narrow, but very deep, division, and having crossed this divide, Chinese potters were able to produce the finest high-fired glazes that the world has ever seen.

In chemical terms the differences between these two types of glazes are small — amounting to the replacement of a small percentage of lime in the earlier glazes with roughly equal amounts of silica and potash — but the gain in depth, subtlety and stability of the glazes was tremendous. This gulf was one that Japanese potters, in particular, found hard to bridge: the vast majority of early Japanese glazes are either lime glazes or truly felspathic glazes. The classic lime-alkali glazes used so successfully in Sung China fall almost exactly midway between these two extremes in the glaze 'spectrum'. How the Chinese managed this great leap forward is very closely linked with the development of porcelain in Southern China.

Fig. 3 Tz'u-chou ware lidded box (height 5·25 inches). White slip over buff clay and iron decoration, Sung dynasty. Fine painting on a good form. Almost all Chinese lids on small boxes, jars and bowls seem to be designed for the whole hand. Where knobs occur they tend to be merely decorative — often emphasizing the fruit-like shapes. *British Museum*

10

2 Chinese Porcelain

The Chinese definition of porcelain

The Chinese word for porcelain, 'tz'u', is applied to three main wares:
Kiangsi porcelain (mainly blue and white), Chekiang celadon, and Fukien
porcelain (known in the West as blanc-de-chine). Kiangsi and Fukien porcelains would pass most of the Western tests for porcelain, but the celadon
wares of Chekiang province have bluish, blue-green or olive-green glazes and
dense, opaque, grey bodies that flash strong rusty-orange colours when re-
oxidized. Most potters would describe them as fine stoneware. However,
when we look further into the technology of these three porcelains we find
that the Chekiang celadons are far closer, technically, to the white porcelains
made in the nearby provinces than to any ordinary stoneware (including
celadons) made elsewhere in China. Chekiang celadon clay is a high-alkali,
high-silica material, almost identical in analysis to white porcelain except
for a slightly higher content of iron and titanium. [6, 7, 8] Practically all
other Chinese stonewares (called 'yao' by the Chinese) are made from low-
silica, low-alkali clays not unlike Western fire clays, and these ordinary
stonewares show none of the super-toughness of the Southern celadons, and
are very prone to produce crazing in the glazes used on them.

Chinese porcelain is essentially a South Chinese material, most of it being
produced within the 'porcelain triangle' made up by the neighbouring provinces of Kiangsi, Chekiang and Fukien. There are some differences in the
raw materials used for porcelain-making in the three provinces: the Kiangsi
potters nowadays use a white clay and a pulverized stone [6]; Chekiang
celadon ware is made from a mixture of white and purple-coloured 'earths'
[7, 8]; and the Fukien kilns use a single pulverized rock that has the characteristics of both clay and stone.[9] Despite these differences it seems
probable that all these clays, stones and semi-plastic stones are derived from
essentially similar rocks.

The important question is whether the four to seven per cent of potash-
plus-soda that is found in the analyses of Sung porcelains and celadon bodies
is mainly introduced by white mica, or by felspar.

12

Modern Chinese porcelain

There is no doubt at all that the ultra-fine variety of potash mica known as sericite supplies most of the alkalis in modern Chinese porcelain and this material is found in both porcelain stone and kaolin. Examples of porcelain raw materials were analysed at the Sèvres factory in France in the late nineteenth century and the highly micaceous character of modern Chinese porcelain was proved for the first time.[10] Similar analyses carried out in Russia in the 1950s with raw materials from Ching-tê Chên (China's thousand-year-old centre for porcelain making), produced the same result — that Kiangsi porcelain was mainly fluxed with mica. Where felspar did occur in the raw materials it was as a secondary flux, and the felspar was of the soda (albite) type rather than the potash type.[11] Where potash felspar was found in these modern Chinese porcelain raw materials it was only as a very minor ingredient in a porcelain stone or clay.

Potash felspar is, of course, the most important flux used in Western porcelains, both in bodies and glazes, and its absence from modern Chinese porcelain is certainly very significant. It raises the question as to why potash felspar is so rarely found in Chinese hard-paste porcelain ingredients.

Sericitization of felspar

The answer to this question seems to be that all the potash felspar originally in the porcelain stones has undergone an unusual type of decomposition that has turned it into a mixture of ultra-fine potash mica and quartz — two ideal ingredients in a hard-paste porcelain body. Most of this decomposition took place millions of years ago and was encouraged by the volcanic nature of the original rocks, for volcanic lavas and ashes cool quickly to produce the kind of fine felspar crystals susceptible to this sericitization. Oddly enough, the soda felspar that was also produced as the lavas cooled is not so easily altered and soda mica is very rare. This subject is made even more complicated by the belief that some *soda* felspar can actually become *potash* mica.[12] Nevertheless, the main result of all this alteration is that the original quartz-felspar rocks turn into mixtures of potash mica (sericite), quartz and soda felspar, but contain practically no potash felspar.

The result of these changes is that the rocks used to make the porcelain 'mixes' in China are actually plastic, after suitable crushing and washing. This is due to the extreme fineness of the potash mica and the similarity of its crystal structure to that of kaolinite (pure clay). It is hard to over-emphasize the value of this plasticity. The nature of porcelain firing within the Chinese range (1250—1350°C) demands a high-silica, high-flux body that leaves very little 'room' for the pure clay that is so necessary for the workability of the porcelain. Western potters have to put up with the negative effect of felspar on plasticity because of its usefulness at white-heat stage. The Chinese potters have, in mica, a material that not only aids plasticity in the making stage but also acts as a strong body-flux at top temperatures. It is also believed that mica in a porcelain body improves the 'stand up' of the ware — its resistance to distortion — and warping of the ware during firing is one of the greatest difficulties encountered in producing hard-paste porcelain.

Sung porcelain and celadon bodies

Bearing in mind that most of the sericitization occurred some millions of years ago; that porcelain has been made at Ching-tê Chên for a thousand years, and that porcelain stone was being dug near to ruined porcelain kilns of the Sung dynasty as recently as 1938[13], what evidence is there, therefore, to suggest that the Chinese have changed their porcelain raw materials since Sung times?

The main evidence is found in one of the most comprehensive scientific studies of Sung porcelains and stonewares made in the West, *Sung Sherds* published in Stockholm in 1963.[5]

The observations that form the basis of the 'potash felspar theory' of Sung porcelains were made by the late Dr Nils Sundius (former State Geologist for Sweden), mainly from microscopic studies of the fired bodies of Sung celadon wares from Chekiang, but also from two examples of white porcelains believed to have been made in Kiangsi. The slides were prepared from sherds collected by the Swedish scholar, Dr Nils Palmgren, in North and South China in the 1930s.

Dr Sundius's general conclusion was that early Chinese celadon bodies and porcelains were prepared from a mixture of pure, and less pure, clays and a pulverized rock that was a natural quartz-felspar mixture. He believed that the felspar in this rock was almost entirely of the potash type. Where mica did occur in these fired sherds he believed that the amounts were 'generally low or moderate . . . and will not be specially mentioned'. However, Dr Sundius did find a mysterious 'scoriaceous quartz' in every sample of Southern Chinese porcelain and celadon that he tested and this was the main difference between the slides of early Chinese porcelains and those of modern Western porcelains that were prepared for comparison. Dr Sundius writes of this 'scoriaceous quartz': 'The grains of it are rich in rounded hollows, filled with a low-refracting glass, probably a melted felspar. The right interpretation of this quartz is a somewhat difficult matter, but it is thought to originate from a fine-grained quartz-felspar rock . . . or a quartz porphyry, used as a fluxing medium for the bodies.'

If Dr Sundius is right, the Chinese have changed their porcelain raw materials radically since Sung times and the earliest South Chinese porcelains were not much different from the hard porcelains made in Europe today. It is, however, just possible to explain away this conclusion by assuming that the 'felspar' crystals found in the slides of the Chinese bodies were *pseudomorphs* of felspar and actually sericite — i.e. the forms of the original felspar crystals had survived their alteration to mica [12]. Such accumulations of ultra-fine mica can behave much like felspar crystals in a firing.

It may be too that the mysterious 'scoriaceous quartz' is simply ordinary quartz attacked by the fluxing action of ultra-fine potash mica. This would create a link between ancient and modern Chinese porcelains, and point to a more acceptable theory for the origins of Chinese porcelains — from decomposed volcanic rocks.

This is a problem that has yet to be fully resolved and, unfortunately, one cannot tell from an oxide analysis of early Chinese porcelain whether potash mica, or potash felspar, has provided the K_2O. By juggling the silica and clay proportions, either, or both minerals, could be fitted into a theoretical mineral 'recipe'. Oxide analyses of Sung porcelains and celadons therefore prove little about the mineralogy of these bodies except that they were low in soda felspar — the high K_2O figure could be allocated to either potash mica, or potash felspar, or to some mixture of the two.

What these analyses do show is that by the end of the Sung dynasty the porcelain makers of Kiangsi, and the celadon potters of Chekiang, were both using bodies with virtually identical ratios of silica, alumina and fluxes — and that this classic balance is almost identical to that found in modern Chinese celadon, and white porcelain bodies. The 'classic' oxide analysis for Chinese porcelain can be summarized by this average fired analysis: silica 70%, alumina 23%, all fluxes 7%. Most of the flux is alkaline (mainly potash, but with some soda). The white porcelains contain about 0·5 to 1·0% iron oxide, while the celadon bodies contain about 2% iron and are only occasionally translucent.

Fig. 4 Tz'u-chou ware vase, Sung dynasty. At first sight this appears to be a thick white glaze over buff stoneware. It is, in fact, a thick *slip* covered with a very thin transparent glaze. Close examination of this type of glaze shows that it is very prone to dense crazing if applied with more than minimal thickness — a fact that must have encouraged the Tz'u-chou potters to concentrate on black and white slips, rather than glazes, to improve their buff stoneware clays. The glaze thickness is usually kept to the minimum necessary to give the wares some gloss while avoiding crazing. The effects of under or over-firing are also far less noticeable in very thin glazes. The white slips used on these wares were almost certainly made from some kind of kaolin, possibly of the less pure secondary type. The glazes used on these white-slipped Tz'u-chou wares seems very much like those used on Ting wares and it is thought that some Northern kilns produced Tz'u-chou, Ting, and even polychrome lead-glazed wares simultaneously. *Victoria and Albert Museum*

3 Development of Early Chinese Celadons and Porcelains

This long digression into the nature of Chinese porcelain clays and stones is an important part of the story of Chinese glazes because it seems very likely that the porcelain body materials were also the main ingredients in the glazes used with them.

The progress in glaze design that took the South Chinese potters from their archaic lime glazes to the finest lime-alkali glazes of the Sung dynasty may be due to nothing more complex than the use of more and more body clay in the glaze recipes, combined with the discovery of deposits of whiter porcelain clays that were richer in alkalis. The increasing amounts of potash and soda found in the purer clays allowed less lime to be used in the glaze recipes, thus vastly improving their quality. These finer and whiter clays also contained less of the earthy impurities of iron and titanium. This was directly reflected in the colours of the best glazes, which changed from dark-green (Han, Fig. 2), to grey-green (Tang, Fig. 5), to light-green, and finally, to almost blue (Sung, Fig. 6) as the amounts of iron and titanium oxides in the clays decreased. These whiter and purer clays were found by the Southern celadon-makers as they explored the wealth of natural porcelain clays found in Chekiang province, particularly in the south of the province in the area around the market town of Lung ch'üan.

Clay + lime = glaze

The idea that the earliest 'proto-porcelain' glazes of South China were made from a simple mixture of the body clay with limestone or lime was first suggested (backed by analyses of glaze and clay) in a short article in Berthold Laufer's rare book *The Beginnings of Porcelain in China.* The article is entitled 'Report on the Technical Investigation of Ancient Chinese Pottery' by H. W. Nichols [3] and it must be one of the most original contributions to the study of Chinese glazes ever written. The ideas put forward not only fit the chemical natures of the clays and glazes, but the technique of mixing lime with the body clay is used today for making celadon glazes in this part of China.

Fig. 5 Tall vase with lightly scratched decoration and clear celadon glaze (height 13 inches). 10th century A.D. Yüeh ware. This must be one of the finest pieces of Yüeh ware in any Western collection and is of the type that inspired the earliest Korean celadons, which are technically similar in clay and glaze. The glaze recipe for this piece may have been the body clay with added lime, and, possibly, some wood ash. Chekiang celadons evolved from lime glazes of this type into thicker and more opaque celadons; the fine drawing seen on this example had to be replaced by broader carving and modelling of the clay to show these later glazes to the best effect. *British Museum*

Mr Nichols' other theory — that the early Chekiang stonewares are the direct ancestors of the later Southern celadons and porcelains — has met with some criticism since Laufer's book was published in 1917 and his term 'proto-porcelain', used to describe the early Chekiang wares, seems rather unpopular with writers on the subject. However, this idea seems likely as a strong family likeness between 'proto-porcelain', Yüeh ware, Lung ch'üan celadon and Kiangsi porcelain was discovered by Dr Sundius in his microscopic and oxide analyses of these wares. Even so, the term 'proto-porcelain' now seems to have been abandoned in favour of 'proto-Yüeh' [14] and the succession of wares from porcellanous stoneware to white porcelain now reads: Proto-Yüeh (Fig. 2) → Yüeh (Fig. 30) → Early Celadon (Fig. 5) → Lung ch'üan celadon (Fig. 6) → Ch'ing-pai porcelain (Fig. 7) → Blue and White porcelain. This succession represents a movement west of about two hundred miles by the centres of ceramic production, and it takes from the start of the Han dynasty to the end of Yüan to run its full course (from about 200 B.C. to A.D. 1368).

Proto-Yüeh wares

The first examples of this ware seem to have been made from a fine, dense and siliceous clay some time in the early Han dynasty and in various parts of Chekiang, although mainly in the north of the province. The clay was fired in a reducing atmosphere and sometimes burnt to an unusual violet-brown colour. The glaze was dark-green, rather fluid and often only applied to rims. It was dull and mottled and was a typical lime glaze. This Proto-Yüeh ware is the ancestor of the Chekiang celadons and the South Chinese porcelains that developed from them. The link between all these wares lies in the chemistry of the raw materials — particularly the siliceous nature of the clays and the natural presence of large amounts of alkaline flux (mostly potash) in the bodies.

The earliest examples of this ware were sometimes too high in iron to make satisfactory stoneware bodies and often showed signs of over-firing, but the use of similar siliceous bodies containing less iron led to the successful development, in the next dynasties, of the famous Yüeh wares that were made from about the third to the tenth centuries A.D.

Yüeh ware

By the time it reached its fullest development in the T'ang dynasty, Yüeh ware had become one of the finest types of pottery ever made in China, with fine grey-green glazes, superb forms and lightly carved and scratched decoration (see Figs. 30 and 5). Yüeh ware also marks the first totally successful exploitation of the unusual Chekiang clays.

Lung ch'üan celadons

Yüeh ware gradually evolved into the transitional celadons of the tenth century, and these in turn became the famous celadons of the Sung dynasty known as Lung ch'üan ware (named after the major market town of the celadon-producing villages of Southern Chekiang). The fine quality and toughness of the Yüeh pottery led to the development of a large trade in the ware and this was continued and enormously expanded with the later Lung ch'üan celadons. These were exported eastwards to Japan, southwards to the Philippines and westwards to the Near East. Southern celadon ware was also distributed throughout China, particularly to the Northern towns where excavation has sometimes shown the Chekiang ware to have been commoner than the native Northern celadons.

A great deal of work is now going on in China to rebuild the old Chekiang celadon industry and both the clays and glazes used for the early and later celadons have been analysed thoroughly as the first stage in re-establishing production of this superb ware. This modern Chinese research is of the greatest interest for the light that it throws on the nature of the materials used to make the finest glazes and earliest porcelains used in this part of China.[7, 8]

Chekiang celadons

One of the most interesting facts revealed in the Chinese studies is that most celadon bodies are — and were — made from mixtures of two types of rather non-plastic clays known as 'white earth' and 'purple-gold' earth. Used alone, the white earths make satisfactory white porcelain bodies, but strangely enough, they were almost invariably mixed with the iron and alkali-rich 'purple-gold' earths to make rather low-firing, grey porcelains that were usually non-translucent and flashed to strong rust-red colours when re-oxidized after reduction. Even when the white earths were used alone — as they appear to have been at the greatest Sung celadon factory at Ta yao — the porcelain was covered with a thick celadon glaze that disguised its translucency (see Fig. 6).

These semi-plastic porcelain 'earths' used for celadons are unfamiliar materials to us in the West. They are not true kaolins or china clays and they probably contain relatively little true clay substance. They are similar

Fig. 6 Lidded jar, Lung ch'üan celadon with thick pale blue glaze with overall crazing (height and width about 5 inches). 12th century A.D. This is an example of the finest type of Southern celadon glaze. Crazing is by no means general with Southern celadons, but the chances of the glazes crazing increases with thickness of application and analyses of some celadon bodies show that they were often just a few per cent too low in silica to avoid crazing completely. *British Museum*

in analysis to the petuntses of Kiangsi province and the more decomposed types of Cornish stone known by the names 'dry white' cr 'buff'.[15] These white earths probably represent yet one stage further on the road from acid rocks to kaolin. The quartz, felspar and mica that are usually washed away in the preparation of English china clays seem to be present in these 'earths' in exactly the right proportion and degree of fineness for making porcelain. (Unfortunately the critical question concerning the proportions of mica to felspar in these 'earths' is not answered by these Chinese studies — they simply state that the alkalis found in analysis are present in micas or felspars.)

It is the indeterminate state between porcelain stone and clay that accounts for the usefulness of white earths and allows them to be used in both bodies and glazes. It is highly probable that many Sung celadon bodies were made by simply adding 15—20% of the purple-gold earth to the white clay, while the celadon glazes could have been made by adding about 20% of a mixture of lime and wood ash to the same (or similar) white clay. This type of body recipe is used today for celadon-ware in Chekiang and the modern celadon glazes are made from a mixture of the body clay with lime and rice-husk ash. These modern glazes are of poorer quality than the Sung celadons and the Chinese suggest that this use of rice-husk ash for glazes is a relatively recent practice in Chekiang, being a Fukien glazing technique and traceable to the eighteenth century when Fukien potters were brought to Chekiang to re-start the Lung ch'üan kilns. The Chinese suggest that pinewood ash was the preferred flux in Sung times because its high potash content would have been useful in the lime-alkali glazes. We can test (but not prove) that Sung celadons were made from mixtures of the 'whiteearth' with pine ash and limestone (or slaked lime), for many analyses exist of white Chekiang clays and limestone used in China today.

Possible Recipe for Sung Celadon Using Chekiang Clay, Limestone, and Pine Ash

	SiO_2	Al_2O_3	Fe_2O_3	CaO	MgO	K_2O	Na_2O	$(K_2O + Na_2O)$	MnO	P_2O_5
				(in percentages)						
Chekiang white earth 80	61·77	13·17	0·4	0·44	0·24	3·8	0·16	(4·96)		
Chekiang slaked lime 10	0·21			5·37	0·08					
Pine ash 10 [16]	2·44	0·97	0·34	3·97	0·44	0·89	0·37	(1·26)	0·27	0·27
Total of oxides (raw)	64·42	14·14	0·77	9·78	0·76	4·7	0·53	(5·23)	0·27	0·27
Celadon glaze (fired)	67·37	14·78	0·8	10·23	0·79	4·9	0·55	(5·45)	0·28	0·28
Real Sung celadon	68·59	14·28	0·73	10·4	0·4	4·97	0·14	(5·01)	not detected	0·14

This imaginary glaze falls well within the very narrow range where the best Sung celadons are found. With eighty per cent 'clay' it should be a good raw glaze and Sung celadon wares often show such typical signs of raw-glazing as parts of the body cut away in fettling the glaze, and the separate glazing beneath the foot with a thinner glaze (turning of the inside of the foot after glazing is a common Eastern raw-glazing practice).[17]

Some white earths tested (theoretically) with this recipe tend to give rather more aluminous celadons than the one above and it is interesting that many genuine analyses of Sung celadons are exactly of this higher-alumina type. (See Analyses of Chinese Glazes on page 79.)

The best 'clays' for making celadon glazes seem to be those that are most similar in analysis to porcelain stones and it may be that the use of porcelain stone itself, rather than the closely related white earths, represents the highest state of development in Southern Sung glazes. The use of porcelain stone would have been more likely to produce the bluest celadons, as this material contains less titanium dioxide than the white and purple earths, and it is titanium that is mainly responsible for the green tones in celadons, because of its modifying effect on the iron oxides in the glazes. Chinese researchers have actually found two caves at the largest Sung celadon kiln site at Ta yao that they believe were Sung glaze-stone mines, suggesting that the rock found there is the same kind of stone as Kiangsi petuntse. Petuntse-lime glazes are still used for glazing Chinese and Japanese porcelains and many Chinese and Japanese porcelain glazes used in the late nineteenth century are almost identical in analysis to thirteenth century Chekiang celadons, although the porcelain glazes were usually applied far too thinly for the similarity to be noticeable.

Early white porcelains

While the Chekiang celadon industry was developing its great productive centres at places like Ta Yao and Ch'i-k'ou, production of true white porcelain (Ch'ing-pai ware) was starting in the neighbouring provinces of Kiangsi and Fukien. Ch'ing-pai ware could be described as 'white celadon' — the designs and decorations are similar to Chekiang celadon, although the scale is usually smaller. Like Chekiang celadon, Ch'ing-pai ware was made and exported in quantity and the links between the two porcelains are very close indeed.

The tremendous growth in the production of blue and white porcelains that developed from these plain Ch'ing-pai wares eventually brought about the decline of the Lung ch'üan celadon factories. There seems to have been a deliberate policy to concentrate porcelain production at Ching-tê Chên (in Kiangsi province) in the Ming dynasty, with the result that after some six centuries of large-scale production, the Lung ch'üan celadon kilns were gradually closed down.

These early white porcelains seem to have varied considerably in plasticity

Fig. 7 Ch'ing-pai porcelain ewer, probably from Ching-tê Chên. 14th century A.D. A late piece of Ch'ing-pai porcelain found in the Philippines and typical of the lively and mass-produced porcelains made for export at the Ching-tê Chên kilns. Blue-white glaze with rust-coloured spots. Wares of this type, but with greyish-blue cobalt spots (rather than brown from iron), are some of the first examples of blue and white porcelains made in China. *Victoria and Albert Museum*

and this may represent different degrees of decomposition of the white earths from the original porcelain stones. In some cases the semi-decomposed stone itself may have been crushed to make the body, as this modern description of preparing porcelain clay at Tehwa in Fukien province suggests:

'The plastic clay body . . . is prepared by grinding and washing a greyish-white weathered rock, which is apparently a natural porcelain mixture. . . . The rock, which is found in various stages of weathering, is sometimes piled on the ground for further weathering, but is often carried in baskets directly to the streams where it is ground.'[9]

We are fortunate in having a description of the early porcelain factories of Ching-tê Chên in Kiangsi province, written by the historian Chiang Ch'i in about 1322,[18] which allows some comparisons to be made between the methods of production suggested for the Chekiang celadons and an actual account of the production of the closely related white porcelains made in the next province.

'The porcelain earth prepared from Chin-k'êng stone is used in the fabrication of the finest porcelain . . . the rocks produced at Hu-k'êng, Ling-pei and Chieh-t'ien being of the second class. . . . It is in the hills of Yu-shan that the mountain brushwood is collected to make the ashes used in the preparation of the glaze. The method adopted is to pile the lime burned from the stone in alternate layers with this brushwood mixed with persimmon (Diospyros) wood, and to burn the two together to ashes. These ashes must be combined with the "glaze earth" brought from Ling-pei before they can be used.'

It is interesting that there is no mention of kaolin in this passage. This is almost always used nowadays, mixed with about 60 per cent petuntse, to make modern Ching-tê Chên porcelain. The Yüan porcelain seems to have been made simply from crushed stone. The account of glaze making shows a deliberate attempt to mix considerable wood ash with the burnt lime, although it is worth remembering that, in terms of weight, about one hundred times as much wood as stone would have had to be burned to achieve an equal weight of usable wood ash and lime; it is likely that wood ash was usually very much the smaller part of these ash-lime mixtures. Whether the 'glaze earth' is the same material as the 'second class' Ling-pei porcelain stone is not clear (see Fig. 8).

Blue and white porcelains

Ching-tê Chên grew to be the greatest centre for porcelain production in China, and from about the time this account was written (1322) to the present day has produced colossal amounts of white, blue-painted, and, later, enamelled porcelains. Practically all ceramic production in South China came to be concentrated at Ching-tê Chên and the provincial Southern kilns suffered accordingly, both by the competition and by the defection of potters to the Kiangsi factories.

Fig. 8 Porcelain bottle decorated with a poem in underglaze copper-red. Made between 1325 and 1350 A.D. This fine bottle is a rare piece of Chinese copper-decorated porcelain, and shows the rather elusive nature of this tricky pigment. After these early experiments, painting with copper oxide was abandoned on Chinese porcelain for some hundreds of years, although the technique continued to be used in Korea. *British Museum*

The following table sums up most of the glazing innovations suggested in the preceding pages. This table proposes that the glazing of stoneware in China could have begun with the use of ash or ash-slag, progressed to clay and ash glazes and then, in South China, to clay and lime glazes. The South Chinese glazes may have evolved naturally — via the Chekiang 'white earths' — from clay-and-lime to porcelain stone-and-lime glazes. The amounts of ash present in most of the Southern glazes were probably considerably lower than the amounts used in Northern glazes.

Possible Development of Early Chinese Celadon and Porcelain Glazes

Possible firing temperature	Dynasty	Type of ware	Type of glaze
About 1200°C	Shang	Coiled stoneware	Most likely pure ash or ash-slag.
About 1200–1240°C	Chou	Thrown stoneware	Glazed by fly-ash in kiln, also by clay and ash.
(South Chinese) About 1200–1240°C	Han	Proto-Yüeh	Mainly body-clay with added lime and maybe some ash. Possibly still some by clay + ash.
About 1220–1250°C	T'ang	Yüeh	As above but with more clay and less lime in recipes.
About 1220–1280°C	Sung	Celadon & Porcelain	Porcelain stone begins to replace porcellanous clay as main ingredient in glaze recipe. Ash still used.
About 1220–1350°C	Sung to present day	Porcelain	Mainly porcelain stone and lime. The amount of ash decreases over the centuries.

Most Shang and Chou wares were made in North China, but the knowledge that clays could be fluxed with ash to make stoneware glazes may have spread southwards to Chekiang province, where at some time the similar fluxing effect of lime or limestone must have been discovered. This material has been used as the main flux in Southern glazes ever since. The use of limestone or slaked lime as a flux to turn porcellanous clays into stoneware or porcelain glazes is, therefore, one of the most vital discoveries in the whole history of Chinese glazes, and almost as important as the discovery of porcelain itself.

Fig. 9 White porcelain ewer with lid (height 8 inches). Northern White ware. Liao dynasty, late 10th or early 11th century. North Chinese white porcelains (as opposed to the cream-coloured Ting wares) are some of the rarest and most fascinating of Chinese wares and the few examples in British museums are masterpieces of their type. They are generally earlier than Ting wares and seem to have been made from high quality kaolins. *Fitzwilliam Museum, Cambridge*

23

4 North Chinese Stonewares and Glazes

The wares of North China have a character of their own that is closely linked with the geology of China north of the Yangtse river and with the early history of the Chinese people. Until the catastrophic overrunning of North China by the Chin tartars in A.D. 1127, the North — and particularly Honan province — was the centre of Chinese civilization, and the finest Northern wares reflect the supremely civilized standards of the Northern Sung period (A.D. 960 to 1126). Their production suffered badly from the flight of the Sung court to South China in 1127, and although some continued to be made after this disaster, they gradually declined in quality and eventually ceased production altogether. The country wares, particularly the black- and white painted and engraved stoneware known as Tz'u-chou ware, fared better; they reflect a virtuosity in throwing and verve in decoration that has survived into modern times (see Figs. 4 and 3).

Although the clays and glazes of South China may be technically better than those used in the North, both the fine and 'country' stonewares of North China show a vitality in making and an imagination in decoration that puts them into a higher order of achievement. Much of this difference must be the result of the different natures of Southern and Northern raw materials. The high flux content of Southern celadons and porcelains makes them much tougher than the Northern stonewares after firing, but they are less plastic in the raw state and from the tenth century onwards most Southern wares show an increasing hardness of profile that must be the result of using purer (but less plastic) raw materials. The Northern potters, by contrast, used 'real' clays that were far more rewarding to the throwers and, in the less 'Imperial' wares, encouraged an earthy and direct style of making (combined with a highly expressive subtlety of form) that can create an impression as powerful as that produced by English medieval wares.

The neat parallels then, that can be drawn between the compositions of South Chinese clays and glazes cannot be extended to take in such fine Northern glazes as Chüns and Northern celadons. The clays used to make these wares were so different in their chemical natures that no satisfactory

Fig. 10 Small Northern celadon plate. Sung dynasty. This plate seems to have been decorated by a mixture of carving and combing, but the potters making Northern celadon also made extensive use of sharply engraved moulds to mass produce 'carved' patterns. It is often difficult to tell which technique has been used. *Victoria and Albert Museum*

Fig. 11 Cup and stand with rust-coloured glazes. North Chinese, perhaps Red Ting ware. 11th—12th century A.D.

The fine white body used for Ting ware was occasionally glazed with black or rust-coloured glazes and even fragments of green Ting ware have been found by the Chinese. This rusty-brown glaze is known by the name 'dead-leaf' in China and is also found on contemporary early porcelains (and stoneware) made in Southern China — mainly on the outside of bowls. Its use at Ching-tê Chên spans hundreds of years and the glaze was still used there in the late nineteenth century. Examples of the Chinese glaze were analysed at Sèvres in the 1880s. *Victoria and Albert Museum*

Fig. 12 Chün plate, pale blue with underglaze copper painting (diameter 7·5 inches). Sung dynasty. The Chün and Northern celadon wares of North China were made for the same kind of markets as the Southern celadons made in Chekiang, but the Northern wares used fine stoneware bodies quite different from the near-porcelains used for Southern celadons. This plate uses broad sweeps of underglaze copper pigment to stain the opalescent blue-white Chün a strong pinkish-red. Heavy reduction is necessary both for the best Chün effects and good reds from copper. The milkiness of the glaze and the 'pinholing' are characteristic of glazes rich in phosphorous oxide — which may be as much as two per cent in Chüns of this type. Many of these Northern Chüns can have analyses similar to Southern celadons. *Victoria and Albert Museum*

glazes could be made from them by using the Southern technique of simply adding small amounts of lime and ash to porcelain 'earths' or stones. North Chinese clays are mainly high-firing aluminous stonewares and they lack the high silica and alkali contents that make the Southern materials such useful glaze ingredients. But despite this vital difference we have to explain the puzzling fact that many Northern Chün glazes that have been analysed are *virtually identical* in their oxide proportions to the best Southern celadons made over six hundred miles to the south-east in Chekiang province. Often the only differences that can be found between the analyses of the two types of glazes are the 0·5 to 1·5% phosphorous pentoxide in the Northern Chüns. It is this small amount of phosphorous that accounts for most of the differences between the glazes and encourages the fascinating 'Chün effect' (Figs. 12 and 13).

It is possible that quartz-felspar rocks provided the alkalis for these Northern glazes, and the similarities in analysis may simply be the result of empirical testing having achieved the same type of 'ideal' glaze — though in a less evolutionary way than happened in the south. The felspar may have been present in some igneous relation to the volcanic porcelain rocks of the South and these quartz-felspar rocks (such as felsite) can have almost identical analyses to porcelain stone, though they are non-plastic after crushing. There is some evidence that some Chüns were biscuit fired before glazing and this would fit the idea that the glazes were made largely from a non-plastic rock.

Only about thirty per cent of felspar would have been needed to provide the five or six per cent of potash + soda found in Northern Chüns. In fact even less would suffice, as most Chüns show a high P_2O_5 content typical of glazes containing ash — and most ashes contain some potash. This means that Chün glazes are not felspathic in the strictest sense, since 50% felspar is usually held to be the lower limit for true felspathic glazes. The Chinese use the term 'lime-alkali' to describe glazes such as Chüns and celadons that contain these moderate amounts of alkalis and such glazes have different characters from the higher-firing true felspathic glazes. It is unlikely (though again just possible) that *all* the alkalis in these Chün glazes were provided by ash. Ash is a rather variable material and the oxide proportions found in these Chüns seem rather too 'good' to be those of ash glazes, and suggest the presence of some acid rock in the recipe to provide the 'bones' of the glaze.

Chün glazes are, in fact, the only North Chinese glazes that have been properly analysed and the other famous Northern glazes — Ting, temmokus, Northern celadons and Imperial 'Ju' ware — can only be discussed technically in terms of their similarities to other glazes that *are* properly understood.

Fig. 13   Chün bottle (6·5 × 6·5 inches) with 'lavender-blue' glaze. 12th to 13th century A.D. This bottle also shows the characteristic pitting and pinholing that enliven these soft-looking, phosphatic, lime-alkali glazes. The clays used for some Chün wares are still unvitrified after stoneware firing and re-oxidize easily to a warm colour, superficially similar to some Southern celadon clays. *Victoria and Albert Museum*

Temmokus

The temmokus of North China, particularly those of Honan province, are fairly easy to theorize about, for we know from work on early Chinese earthenwares that the red and yellow-firing clays from the flood plains and loess regions of North China begin to melt into black glass about 1100°C. These clays would make good, if slightly dull, black glazes if fired in an oxidizing atmosphere in the high stoneware range (1280 to 1310°C). Small amounts of ash or limestone added to the clays would improve the gloss of these black glazes — if this was desired. A grey-firing Chou dynasty clay from the Tz'u-chou region of North China (analysed for Dr Sundius)[19] would make a dullish-black stoneware glaze at stoneware temperatures, but with less than ten per cent ash or lime added to it, its analysis would be virtually the same as that of the Albany slip clays of America. Albany slips have often been described as being very similar to North Chinese temmokus and they share many characteristics with them, particularly in the way the glazes show a light-brown, glossy transparency where thinly applied, but become a fine opaque black where dipped more thickly. Many Honan temmoku bottles and jars show deliberate use of this effect (Fig. 14), and the contrast is most pronounced when the firing has been oxidizing or neutral.

Ting ware

Ting ware is one of the most unusual ceramic materials made in China and nothing quite like it has been made there since its production ceased about A.D. 1300. The fascination of Ting ware lies less in the thin, brilliant, faintly yellowish glaze, than in the fine near-white body beneath it.

If it were not for the well-documented fact that some pieces of Ting ware are translucent this clay could be explained as an ultra-refined, light-coloured stoneware, fired in an oxidizing atmosphere to avoid the greyness typical of reduced stonewares (but not true porcelains). However, the orange or yellowish translucency in strong light of some Ting wares makes it some kind of porcelain — but obviously a very different type from that made in the South.

Compared with the wealth of detailed analyses of Southern celadon and porcelain materials, the technical information published on Ting wares is very sparse indeed, being confined to two analyses of Ting bodies and no analyses at all of Ting glazes. The two body analyses are as follows:

	SiO_2	Al_2O_3	Fe_2O_3	TiO_2	MgO	CaO	Na_2O	K_2O	$(K_2O + Na_2O)$
Sung Ting body (1)	61·72	32·12	0·55	0·69	1·12	1·04	0·92	1·31	(2·23)
Sung Ting body (2)	60·0	32·78	2·07	1·61	0·45	0·79	0·16	1·66	(1·82)

These analyses show that these particular examples of Ting ware have basically the same type of rather aluminous bodies as the other Northern wares, such as Chün ware, Northern celadon and Northern temmoku, and analysis (2) can be taken as typical for the bodies of most of these wares. Analysis (1), however, contains a most unusual amount of magnesia and it has been suggested that the earliest white porcelains made in the same district as the later Ting wares had dolomite added to their bodies to produce translucency (as opposed to the felspars and micas that produced translucency in the Southern porcelains).[14] It is possible that the use of magnesia and/or lime as a body flux continued in the Ting wares and the translucency sometimes found in Ting wares may be due to this practice. In some cases the alkaline earths (CaO, MgO) may have merely hardened the body — the amounts used, or the firing temperatures employed, being too low to give genuine translucency.

The presence of lime and magnesia in analysis (1) may or may not have been deliberate, but both oxides are known to be very efficient body fluxes and one per cent of lime is thought to be the equivalent of 10 per cent of felspar above 1100°C.[20] Lime is, in fact, rather too efficient as a body flux and shows the same sudden melting characteristics in clays as it does in glazes. Lime was once widely used in both hard and soft eighteenth-century Western porcelains but it caused high kiln losses through warping and collapse of the wares and was abandoned once the superior qualities of felspar became known. Magnesia has the same efficiency as lime but is supposedly less liable to cause distortion.

The greatest trouble experienced by the Ting ware potters seems to have been the warping of the wares in the firing. They overcame this difficulty by firing most flat wares and bowls upside down on unglazed rims which had to be finished off after the firing by adding bands of copper, silver, or even gold. The tendency of Ting ware to warp badly might lend support to the idea that lime or magnesia was used in the clay as a flux, although the evidence for this is still very slight at the moment.

On most Ting wares the glaze is extremely thin, but has a peculiar brilliance almost like a lead glaze. This, however, is also a characteristic of glazes containing considerable lime and, especially, magnesia. The distinctness of the famous 'tear marks' on Ting glazes suggests that the glazes are of a lime or lime-magnesia composition — as does their somewhat glue-like character, which is typical of oxidized, high-fired lime glazes.

Ju ware

Shortly before the collapse of the Northern Sung dynasty in 1127, Ting ware became unfashionable for court use and its place was taken by the rarest of Chinese classic wares known as Ju-yao. This ware has great simplicity of form and a glaze that is reminiscent of that used on Chün ware, although when the two wares are seen side by side the Chün glazes look distinctly flashy by comparison. As with Northern celadon and Kuan ware, the greyness of the stoneware body darkens the glaze, producing a more reserved impression than that given by the Southern celadons. Like Northern Chüns and Southern Kuan glazes, Ju glazes are thought to contain about 0·5% phosphorous pentoxide.[5] The phosphorous creates slight opalescence and adds a luminous depth to the blue-green or blue-grey colours of the Ju glazes, which are usually crazed. The very refractory stoneware clay used for Ju ware has led to the body being described as earthenware. This may be

Fig. 14 North Chinese black-glazed bottle from Honan province (height 10 inches). Sung dynasty and excavated at Ch'ing-ho Hsien, Hopei province. This magnificent example of Northern temmoku seems to be glazed with a low-alkali aluminous, iron-glaze like the Albany slip clays of North America, and fired in an oxidizing atmosphere. Typical of this type of glaze is its brown transparency where thin, compared with its rich black opacity when used thickly. In the finest fluted temmokus of this type the body is often dipped in white slip before the fluting is carried out in order to give greater contrast between the thinly-glazed ribs and the black glaze. *Sotheby and Co., London*

29

Fig. 15 Ting ware bowl (diameter 9 inches). Sung dynasty.
Fine pieces, such as this bowl, make Ting ware a porcelain in spirit, if not in substance. Very little is known about the chemistry of Ting wares, which can sometimes show a pinkish or orange translucency. The most important questions to be answered are the nature of the fluxes used to produce this translucency, and whether the clay generally used for Ting ware is a kaolin or simply a refined stoneware. There seem to be many types of Ting ware, some much whiter than others, and by no means all of them are translucent. *British Museum*

strictly accurate, but, as the glaze was probably fired between about 1220 and 1260°C it is less confusing to treat it as a stoneware. The composition of the Ju ware glazes can be estimated as being somewhere between Kuan glazes and Chün glazes (i.e. in the lime to lime-alkali range) and they tend to show the typical variations wrought on this type of glaze by differences in firing temperatures.

Northern celadons

Such similarities as exist between Northern and Southern celadons are mainly confined to the glazes, for the bodies are known to be very different, with Chekiang (Southern) celadon being made from an impure porcelain, while the Northern celadon potters used a fine natural stoneware clay, low in flux and high in alumina.[5] Northern stoneware clays contain enough iron and titanium oxides to make them fire rather grey in reduction, and it is this grey tone in the reduced clay that is so obvious beneath the glassy, olive-green, Northern celadon glazes. (Strangely enough, small amounts of iron *alone* are not so likely to make clays fire grey in reduction: many white Chinese porcelains have iron contents in the 1·0 to 1·5% range typical of the Northern clays.)[21]

It is impossible to know just how similar these Northern celadon glazes are to the glazes used in Chekiang at the same time until some analyses are made of the Northern glazes. From the rather second-hand evidence of the related Northern Chüns (which have been analysed) they may be very similar indeed. It can be assumed, simply from their appearance, that they contain more iron than the Chekiang celadons (say about 1·5% iron oxides) and their olive tone suggests a titanium content possibly as high as 0·5%.

Tz'u-chou ware

The last type of North Chinese stoneware to be considered is Tz'u-chou ware — a very broad term that takes in most of the black, white, and black-and-white ordinary stonewares made in North China. The 'temmoku' variety of this ware has already been mentioned, and the technique of carving through the black glaze to show the grey or buff stoneware body beneath was also used on the white Tz'u-chou wares, although in this case the carving was through a thick white slip subsequently covered by a thin, clear glaze.

It is often the case with ceramics that the poorer the fabric the better the decoration, and the incised and slip-painted designs on Tz'u-chou wares transform what, in most cases, are rather poor clays and ill-fitting glazes into some of the most exciting and impressive pottery ever made (see Figs. 4 and 3).

5 Chemistry of Chinese and Japanese Glazes

Behind every aesthetic aspect of Far Eastern glazes lies a technical fact and this is an incentive to tackle the strings of figures that are the technical expressions of these fascinating glazes. Analyses of Oriental glazes take us directly to those narrow, but extraordinarily fertile, areas of glaze composition that have provided the Chinese, Japanese, and very probably the Koreans with their best glazes for hundreds of years. These analyses allow us to re-create the glazes and also provide many clues to the fundamental principles of glaze construction.

The *technical* soundness that these analyses also represent has long been recognized by Western potters, and in the late nineteenth century many European porcelain factories began to re-design bodies and glazes to bring them closer in analysis to Far Eastern wares. The greatest fault with Western work on these lines has been the tendency to 'copy' these Eastern clays and glazes with only the purest Western raw materials. The result, in most cases, is that only the *technical* virtues have survived and the true character of the original Eastern porcelains and glazes has been 'rationalized' out of existence.

Because of the risk of losing all the natural variety provided by those 'impurities' always found in Oriental glazes, some way has to be found of retaining them when re-creating the glazes with Western raw materials. Not only do we need to understand the parts played by all the minor oxides that are found in analyses of Eastern glazes, but also how to introduce these oxides into our re-created glazes in the same amounts as in the original glazes. This demands a method of calculation that is both subtle and accurate, and unfortunately, these are not the strongest points of the conventional method of glaze-making (the Seger or molecular method).

However, there is another method of expressing, comparing and calculating glazes that uses no molecular weights but works directly with the *real weights* of the oxides shown in the analyses of the clays and glazes, and with the oxides found in the raw materials used to re-create them. This method is known as the Percentage Method and is simpler, more accurate, and more flexible than the Seger method. It is also much easier to under-

Fig. 16 Stoneware jar (height about 10 inches), 6th—7th century A.D. This powerful jar is of a Northern type and the 'thumbed' decoration serves to prevent the glaze from running down and sticking the pot to its support in the kiln. The fact that the glaze may contain considerable ash is suggested by its 'Chün-like', blue opalescence where it has thickened in the ridges. The overall colour of the glaze is watery-green. *British Museum*

stand how glazes 'work' if they are presented in the percentage style. The percentage style of expressing glazes is, in fact, the way in which the majority of Oriental glazes are described in the archaelogical and technical papers, where lists of oxides-by-weight are expressed as percentages of the fired glazes. But rather than accept all this on trust it is still useful to know exactly why the Seger method is less suitable for this kind of work, and some of the reasons can be found by studying the logic behind the Seger system.

Ultimate analysis versus the Seger (molecular) method

The Seger method of glaze calculation probably owes its creation to the fact that most raw materials used in Western fine ceramics are so pure that they can be represented as *minerals* rather than *rocks* (which are mixtures of minerals). Thus the felspars, china clays, whiting and flints are so free from contamination by other minerals that they can be represented by their chemical formulae. The felspars can therefore be treated as pure albite or orthoclase; the china clays as kaolinite; the whiting and limestone as calcium carbonate; and flint and quartz as pure silica. Any analyses that might be made of these pure raw materials would be found to be very similar to the analyses characteristic of the pure minerals. This fact must have prompted Dr Hermann Seger to hit on the original idea of representing *glazes* as molecular formulae too.

Although glazes are not actually found in the neat molecular proportions characteristic of natural minerals they can be manipulated mathematically to make a 'formula', and this can be arranged to take the same form as, for example, potash felspar (orthoclase): $1 \cdot 0$ K_2O, $1 \cdot 0$ Al_2O_3, 6 SiO_2. A glaze that contains the following oxides in real percentage weights — 67 SiO_2, 13 Al_2O_3, $12 \cdot 5$ CaO, $6 \cdot 0$ K_2O and $1 \cdot 3$ MgO — becomes, for the purpose of calculation by the Seger method, the following 'formula':

$$K_2O \quad 0 \cdot 2$$
$$CaO \quad 0 \cdot 7 \quad\quad 0 \cdot 4 \; Al_2O_3 \quad SiO_2 \; 3 \cdot 5 \text{ (A cone 7–9 porcelain glaze)[2]}$$
$$MgO \quad 0 \cdot 1$$

The Seger (or molecular) formula can be seen here as somewhat many-headed, with three oxides sharing the place occupied by the '$1 \cdot 0$ K_2O' in the felspar formula. The idea of setting the fluxes together and making them add up to one is to make it easier to compare the ratios of alumina (Al_2O_3) to silica (SiO_2) in different glazes, as expressed in the Seger method.

Having brought the percentage list of oxides-by-weight to this 'molecular' state (a fairly complicated process), it is relatively easy to work out the 'parts' of complete molecules (representing pure raw materials) that 'fit' the Seger formula: thus $0 \cdot 2$ mol. parts of potash felspar provide the $0 \cdot 2$ K_2O, as well as $0 \cdot 2$ of the Al_2O_3 and $1 \cdot 2$ of the SiO_2. We work by a process of sub-division until we end up with a list of decimal parts of complete molecules of different minerals or raw materials. This list — although accurately reflecting the Seger formula of the glaze — is of no use until it is changed from molecular proportions to *real* proportions by weight. This is done by multiplying each decimal part of the 'ingredient-as-molecule' by the *formula weight* particular to that mineral or raw material. The formula weight is the sum total of all the atomic weights of all the atoms in each 'raw-material-as-molecule'.

All this sounds complicated, but it is roughly the equivalent of having to change all our money from pounds into francs because all the goods in the shops are marked in francs. To get any idea of what we have spent we have to re-convert back from francs to pounds, just as we have to re-convert back from molecular to real weights to achieve a usable recipe.

Expressed like this, the Seger method raises the obvious question: why not have the prices in pounds in the first place? Or, more exactly, why turn these glazes into molecular formulae anyway, rather than calculate directly with the oxides in the glazes, and the oxides in the raw materials used to make the glazes? It is, in fact, quite possible to do this, and this is the method adopted in this book. The percentage method is particularly suitable for dealing with Far Eastern glazes as the materials used to make the glazes were *not* pure felspars and clays, and the best results come from using natural and 'impure' raw materials to re-create them. If the Seger method is used with this type of glaze and glaze-ingredient it becomes a very much more complicated and unwieldy process that demands about twice as much calculation as the percentage method. Another serious drawback of the Seger method is that the procedure of translating from the list of oxides-by-weight to the Seger formula destroys the highly revealing pattern of the percentage expression. This changes such easily understandable (and important) figures as $1\cdot0\%$ Fe_2O_3, or $0\cdot5\%$ P_2O_5 to $0\cdot04$ Fe_2O_3 (mol.) and $0\cdot01$ P_2O_5 (mol.). Also, because it expresses the silica and alumina in terms of a ratio, the Seger method obscures a most useful fact provided by a percentage analysis: the exact percentage by weight of silica in the fired glaze. For instance, the 'formulae' for the potash felspar and the stoneware glaze just given suggest that the felspar with $6\cdot0$ SiO_2 (mol.) contains more silica than the porcelain glaze with $3\cdot5$ SiO_2 (mol.). In fact, the porcelain glaze contains *more* silica (at 67% SiO_2) than the pure potash felspar with only $64\cdot8\%$ SiO_2. The more one studies these two methods the more one comes to suspect that the Seger method actually provides less information about a glaze than does a percentage analysis.

General guides for understanding (and creating) stoneware glazes of the 'Far Eastern' type

Bearing in mind that the glass-forming oxide *silica* provides the bulk of the glazes, the *fluxes* reduce the melting point of silica from $1710°C$ to about $1200°C$, and the *alumina* acts as a 'stiffener' to prevent the glaze running off the pots, the following guides illustrate the typical proportions that these three glaze components tend to display in most Far Eastern glazes. The guides can also be applied to a great number of Western stoneware glazes that are of the 'Far Eastern' type.

1. Almost all Far Eastern stoneware glazes contain between 60—74% silica if they are to mature in the temperature range 1220—1310°C. The higher these glazes are fired within this range, the more silica they need if they are not to become glassy and prone to run.

2. Ideal silica contents for glazes of this type:

> 67% silica for cone seven (1230°C)
> 68% silica for cone eight (1250°C)
> 69% silica for cone nine (1280°C)
> and 70—71% silica for cone ten (1300°C)

(If a 'Far Eastern' type of glaze has a silica content different from the ideal figure suggested for its maturing temperature, it can be considered a high or low-silica glaze, according to the amount it differs from the ideal).

3. The maturing temperature of these glazes depends more than anything else on the *sum totals of the silica and alumina percentages*. The following silica and alumina totals will give good glazes within the following temperature ranges if the silica contents are within the limits suggested in 1:

> Cones six to eight — silica + alumina 73—80% of total glaze
> Cones seven to nine — silica + alumina 78—82% of total glaze
> Cones eight to ten — silica + alumina 80—85% of total glaze

4. As the maturing temperatures for 'Far Eastern' glazes depend mainly on the *total* amount of silica and alumina, a high alumina figure does not necessarily mean a high maturing temperature. A high-alumina glaze with a low silica percentage can still run badly if the SiO_2 + Al_2O_3 total is low, because the silica also plays a part in hardening the glaze. Seventeen per cent alumina represents the normal upper limit in Chinese glazes, and the commonest amounts of alumina in these glazes are found to be between ten and fifteen per cent.

These guides have been abstracted from analyses of about fifty Far Eastern glazes and an equal number of Western glazes of a similar type. Guides 1, 3, and 4, cover such glazes as mirror-blacks, ash-glazes, Chüns and copper-reds as well as higher firing glazes, such as natural temmokus and Kakis. Guide 2, is more concerned with 'good' glazes, i.e. glazes of very high technical quality. (The best celadon and porcelain glazes of China and Japan come into this category.) The figures suggested for the silica contents of glazes of this type might seem rather rigid, but they are figures that recur time and again in analyses of fine glazes maturing in this range. Guide 3, is probably the most useful of all, for not only does it give a good idea of the likely maturing temperature of a glaze from one look at its analysis, but also allows glazes to be designed from first principles that will almost certainly mature at the temperatures intended.

The fluxes

The 15—30% of oxides remaining, after the silica and alumina have been counted, can be described collectively as 'the fluxes'. These five fluxes, iron oxide, lime, magnesia, soda and potash are found together in almost every Far Eastern glaze. The alkalis, soda and potash, however, are marginally more efficient as fluxes than lime and magnesia (the alkaline earths), but this difference is not enough to upset the general maturing limits suggested in 3. Glazes maturing at about 1200°C need 25 to 30% mixed fluxes, while at about 1300° only 15—20% are needed.

The last two oxides to be considered in these very general remarks about glaze construction occur in rather small amounts in Far Eastern glazes, but after iron oxide, are the most important suppliers of 'quality' to the glazes. They are titanium and phosphorous oxides.

Typical proportions of TiO_2 and P_2O_5 in glazes are usually well below one per cent, but so powerful is the effect of titanium that 0·2% TiO_2 is a very significant amount. Both oxides profoundly affect the colour and character of glazes containing small amounts of iron: titanium makes these glazes greener in reduction and yellower in oxidation, while phosphorous produces millions of bubbles in a glaze that are reluctant to disperse even with longer soaking or greater heat (see Figs. 12 and 13). In the right conditions phosphorous also encourages the rather mysterious 'Chün' effect which creates a blue opalescence within low-iron glazes. Titanium and phosphorous oxides are *not* fluxes, so when they occur in useful amounts in stoneware glazes they should be counted on the $SiO_2 + Al_2O_3$ side of the 'balance'.

Chinese glazes in detail

1. *Oriental glazes of the 'ideal' or 'lime-alkali' type*
About half of the fifty or so analyses of ancient and modern Far Eastern glazes collected for this book are so similar to each other that they suggest that the world of Far Eastern glazes contains a truly classic balance of oxides so perfect that it has provided Oriental potters with their finest glazes for at least a thousand years. This 'classic' glaze was first used in China in about A.D. 900—1000 and formed the basis of most Lung ch'üan celadon glazes, many Northern Chüns, and very many porcelain glazes, both Chinese and Japanese (see Figs. 6, 8 and 12). It also represents a balance of oxides so *technically* ideal that it is used on much modern, industrial, Western stoneware and porcelain where a glaze maturing in the range 1250—1300°C is needed. This glaze has a particularly long maturing range and the low-iron type will give

a fine, white, opaque glaze at cone seven (1230°C) passing through various stages of clarity to give an excellent transparent porcelain glaze up to 1300°C. Small changes in the minor oxides (iron, titanium manganese and phosphorous) in this classic glaze will give all the celadon colours from olive-green to pale blue, as well as a number of superb Chüns. Most Oriental porcelain glazes are simply low-iron versions of this glaze applied thinly and fired higher than ordinary celadons to allow the cobalt painting beneath the glaze to show through.

Typical ancient and modern examples of this 'ideal' glaze are shown below:

	SiO_2	Al_2O_3	Fe_2O_3	TiO_2	CaO	MgO	K_2O	Na_2O	$(K_2O + Na_2O)$	P_2O_5
Lung ch'üan celadon (Sung)[5]	68·6	14·28	0·73	0·02	10·4	0·4	4·97	0·14	(5·03)	0·14
Chinese porcelain glaze (about 1880) [10]	69·43	14·35	0·78		9·68	0·44	3·3	2·12	(5·42)	
Japanese porcelain glaze (late 19th C.) [22]	68·5	14·3	0·43		10·6		4·62	1·24	(5·86)	0·43
Western porcelain glaze. (modern)[2]	69·6	13·7			10·5	1·1	4·6		(4·6)	
North Chinese Chün (12th C. A.D.)	67·0	14·12	1·68	0·21	9·95	0·67	5·0		(5·0)	

The remarkable similarities between these Far Eastern glazes raises the question of how such consistency could have been maintained for so long without the aids of analysis. The likely explanation for the two Oriental porcelain glazes and the Sung celadon seems to be that all three recipes probably made use of about 80% porcelain stone (or porcelain 'earth') as the basis of the glaze, with the remaining 20% or so of the recipe provided by lime and/or ash. But how the Northern Chün comes to have such a similar analysis is certainly something of a mystery, for these types of porcelain stones and earths are not found in North China. The answer to this may be that a similar (but non-plastic) rock such as a white granite was used instead. The modern Western glazes that use the same balance of oxides probably owe their origins in the main part to the interest shown in Eastern glazes by Dr Hermann Seger in the nineteenth century.

Although it is possible to make some guess as to *how* this glaze was made in China and Japan, it is harder to understand *why* it works so well. The wide maturing range of this glaze suggests that it represents some kind of eutectic mixture, or, possibly, a mixture of two 'eutectics'. In fact a 50:50 mixture of the 1170° lime eutectic and the mixture of orthoclase and quartz represented by the molecular formulae K_2O, Al_2O_3, $9 SiO_2$ [2] gives the following percentage analysis.

SiO_2 67·7 Al_2O_3 14·27   CaO 11·6 K_2O 6·35

While this is very similar to the ideal glaze, the 6·35 K_2O would have been just out of reach of the Sung potters with their low-alkali raw materials. It is possible, however, that the 'classic' Far Eastern glaze was an approximation to this theoretical mixture.

A less abstract answer as to why the oxides in the best Chinese and Japanese glazes fall within such narrow limits might be found by studying the effects of altering the amounts of some oxides while keeping others constant.

Effects of altering any oxides in the 'ideal' type of Oriental glaze
Silica: *less* silica would make the glazes prone to crazing, glassier in character and prone to run. *More* silica and the glaze would be underfired and eventually become white and opaque. (Such an effect is used deliberately by Kiangsi porcelain makers to produce a particularly white ground for later enamelling at a lower temperature. This type of glaze is too opaque for use with under-glaze cobalt and is made by simply reducing the amount of lime in the glaze recipe in relation to the porcelain stone, thus automatically increasing the silica content of the glaze. The white opacity is mainly caused by undissolved silica.)
Alumina: *less* alumina would make the glaze clearer, less full of 'body', and by diminishing the millions of bubbles trapped in a 'stiff' glaze would badly affect the jade-like character of celadons. (The clearer porcelain glazes are achieved with the same base celadon glaze by firing them higher and applying them more thinly.) *More* alumina would raise the maturing temperature, produce a matt surface and tend to dull the true colour of the glaze.
Lime: *less* lime would increase the ratio of alkalis to lime but the effects would only show if the glaze were fired higher to offset the loss in flux. *More* lime would affect the 'ideal' two parts lime to one part alkali balance, making the glaze either duller or glassier, depending on the firing temperature, and the transitional stage between these two states would be smaller than in true celadons. More lime would make this glaze more similar to the pre-Sung celadons.
The alkalis: *less* potash and soda would have the same result as adding more lime, although at a higher temperature. *More* alkali would give a more brilliant glaze at a lower temperature but also increase the risk of crazing. It can be seen from these remarks that the 'classic' glaze does need to stay within its rather narrow limits for its particular type of excellence.

When we come to look at other Chinese glazes in detail they can be conveniently divided into lime glazes, alkaline glazes, phosphatic glazes and iron glazes. This does not mean that lime, the alkalis, phosphorous, or iron are the main oxides in the analyses, but it is simply a useful way of classifying glazes that are well above average in these particular oxides and which also owe much of their character to the presence of these oxides.

2. *Lime glazes*

The vast majority of light-coloured Chinese stoneware glazes are fluxed by some combination of lime with potash and soda, with lime almost always taking the larger share.

The traditional way to prepare lime for glazes in China is to burn limestone with wood or bracken, slake the nearly pure calcium oxide (CaO) thus formed with water, and mix the slaked lime with clay or porcelain stone (and sometimes rice-husk ash) to make the glaze. This burning of the stone saves crushing it and the slaking of the quick-lime liberates considerable energy creating fine calcium hydroxide powder double the volume of the original rock. Another important advantage of burning rather than crushing is that lime is less active in a glaze if it has already been burned, and gives a clearer glaze with less bubbling as there is no disassociation of CO_2 when the glaze is melting. This is an important point when trying to imitate Chinese glazes as the materials most commonly used to provide CaO in Western glazes (limestone and whiting) do undergo this active decomposition at high temperatures. Results nearer to the effects that the Chinese achieve with slaked lime can come from using *wollastonite* in a glaze instead

Fig. 17   Celadon glazed teapot by the author (height 6·5 inches, overall width 11 inches). Pale green celadon on porcellanous stoneware, fired to about 1240°C in an oil-fired kiln (Glaze No. 2). The use of wollastonite rather than whiting in this glaze lessens the risks from smoke staining due to heavy reduction in oil-fired kilns, although this is less of a problem in gas-fired kilns. The body recipe uses 80 parts SM ball clay (not SMD) and 20 parts nepheline syenite. The recipe was created from analyses of South Chinese celadon bodies and porcelains by using the 'simultaneous' method of calculation described on page 57.

of whiting (see Fig. 17). (Wollastonite is a calcium silicate, with a typical analysis of 51% SiO_2 and 47% CaO.) When wollastonite is used to replace whiting in a glaze, the quartz or flint content of the glaze must be adjusted to allow for the extra silica.

Of the many kinds of limestone available to them, the Chinese tend to use those that are low in such impurities as clay and silica to burn for glazes. Limestones containing more than a few per cent of such impurities often have 'hydraulic' properties (meaning that they set solid under water), and this is obviously a drawback with a glaze material.

Kuan glazes

Although lime glazes are usually associated with ancient or country stoneware, there is one exceptional type of lime glaze — used on the Kuan ware of the Southern Sung dynasty — that must be one of the most sophisticated glazes ever used in China. In their general appearance Kuan glazes seem to lie somewhere between Northern Chüns and Southern celadons (see Fig. 18), but the one analysis of a Kuan glaze that is available is higher in lime than either of these glazes and more like the transitional celadons of the Five Dynasties period (A.D. 907—960).

Fig. 18 Small Kuan ware vase. South Chinese, 12th—13th centuries A.D. This vase shows the typical Kuan characteristics of thick glazes, heavy crazing, a dark body and a somewhat archaic shape. The one genuine analysis of a South Chinese Kuan glaze showed it to be of the lime glaze type, containing a small amount of phosphorous oxide. *Victoria and Albert Museum*

Analysis of a Kuan glaze and body (Southern Sung period)[5]

	SiO_2	Al_2O_3	TiO_2	Fe_2O_3	CaO	MgO	K_2O	Na_2O	$(K_2O + Na_2O)$	P_2O_5
Kuan glaze	63·0	15·31	0·03	1·08	14·54	1·02	4·0	0·16	(4·16)	0·52
Kuan body	64·4	28·72	1·1	1·98	0·26	0·48	2·48	0·24	(2·72)	

The phosphorous content of this Kuan glaze is more typical of North Chinese Chüns than Southern celadons, and Kuan ware is often described as a Northern ware that had its production transferred to the new Southern capital of Hang-chou some fourteen years after the disastrous overrunning of the Northern capital in A.D. 1127. Although Southern Kuan ware was made in the great celadon-producing province of Chekiang, it used a low-silica stoneware body that is similar in analysis to the Northern stonewares. This clay used for Kuan ware may be related to the 'purple-gold earths' added to the white chekiang celadon clays.

There does not seem to have been a ware exactly like Kuan-yao made in North China, although some examples of the very rare Ju ware do resemble it. Southern Kuan has a smooth, thick, lustrous pale grey or blue-grey glaze — its 'precious' character emphasized by the rather decorative, and often deliberately archaic forms that characterize the more 'Imperial' wares of the Southern Sung dynasty. The high phosphorous total in the analysis may mean that a fair amount of wood ash was used in the recipe, and the very low titanium figure suggests that the body clay was not one of the glaze ingredients and incidentally accounts for the rareness of green tones in Kuan glazes (another sign of 'Imperial' quality). Kuan ware was probably fired below 1250°C and may have been cooled quickly as this is one way of preventing excessive dullness in a slightly underfired lime-glaze. Broken pieces of Kuan ware often show a glaze thickness greater in total than the thickness of the body. In most stonewares this would result in shattering from excessive strain on the body from the glaze, but the low silica content of both glaze and body in Kuan ware prevents this.

Kuan glazes show some resemblances to true felspathic glazes such as the rather unattractive 'crackle' glazes used on some late nineteenth-century Chinese porcelains. These modern crackle glazes were probably fired to at least 50°C higher than the Kuan glazes and the 'crackle' effect is caused by a high potash and soda content in the glazes, rather than the low silica percentages in body and glaze that account for the similar effect in Kuan glazes. (These late 'crackle' glazes are some of the very few truly felspathic Chinese glazes and were made from petuntses unusually rich in soda felspar.[10] Some celadon glazes used at Ching-tê Chên in the 1950s also seem to be felspathic,[6] but this is probably an example of Japanese technical influence rather than native Chinese innovation.)

By far the greatest part of the story of Chinese glazes is concerned with the gradual evolution of lime glazes (mostly low silica) to lime-alkali glazes (higher silica, less lime, more alkalis). The most typical features of this development (in chemical terms) can be illustrated by the following table that describes the evolution of Chinese glazes over about two thousand years, from the Han dynasty to the present day.

Type of glaze	SiO_2%	Al_2O_3%	CaO%	$K_2O + Na_2O$%	Fe_2O_3%	Maturing Temp.
Archaic glazes, Proto-Yüeh, etc. *High-lime glazes*	54—58	15—17	15—23	3—4	4—6	1200°C
Early celadons and Kuan glazes *Lime glazes*	59—64	15—17	13—16	3—4	1—2	1230°C
Ideal celadons, Chüns and porcelain glazes *Lime-alkali glazes*	65·5—70	14—15	9—11	5—6·5	1—2	1250°C
Some modern Chinese and Japanese celadons *Felspathic glazes*	69—72	12—14	5—9	7—12	1·5—2	1290°C

The most important changes took place in the first thousand years A.D. and most of the stoneware and porcelain glazes used in China from the Sung dynasty to the present day have been of the lime or lime-alkali types. The last class (felspathic glazes) is a relatively new type of glaze in China and its introduction may be due to Japanese, or even Western, influence.

3. *Felspathic and alkaline glazes*

Chinese glazes made in the greatest periods (T'ang, Five Dynasties, Sung and Yüan) are *not* notably high in alkalis, but the amounts that are found in the best glazes of the time are entirely adequate to transform the earlier lime glazes into those rich and lustrous glazes known as lime-alkali glazes. An equally important part of this improvement was a slight increase in the silica content of the glazes, giving them more substance and resistance to the effects of slight over-firing. The classic balance of lime to alkalis in these Chinese glazes is almost exactly 2:1, and a typical glaze of the best type might contain 11% lime and 5·5% alkalis.

The misunderstanding that has led to the finest types of early Chinese glazes being described as 'felspathic' is, in fact, quite understandable, because there does happen to be a particular type of felspathic glaze that is fired to about 50°C higher than a typical lime-alkali glaze and has a strong superficial similarity to these early glazes, although it is of a rather different chemical make-up. These felspathic glazes are above average in silica content, but below average in alumina; whereas lime-alkali glazes are slightly below average in silica content and above average in alumina. Finally, a lime-alkali glaze usually contains about twice as much lime as it will potash and soda; whereas a true felspathic glaze will often contain more potash and soda than lime. All these differences can be seen in the three typical glazes analysed below. The first is a Sung lime-alkali celadon, while the other two are modern Japanese and Chinese felspathic celadons:

Lime-alkali Celadon Compared with Felspathic Celadons

	SiO_2	Al_2O_3	Fe_2O_3	TiO_2	CaO	MgO	K_2O	Na_2O	$(K_2O + Na_2O)$	Maturing temperature
Sung celadon[8]	66·33	14·28	1·0	0·03	11·34	1·17	4·35	1·0	(5·35)	1250°C
1930 Japanese celadon[23, 24]	73·3	12·3	1·67		5·9		7·2		(7·2)	1290°C
1956 Chinese celadon[6]	71·0	13·5	1·95	0·18	5·0	0·46	4·4	3·8	(8·2)	1290°C

The felspathic Chinese celadon, used at Ching-tê Chên in the 1950s, is very different from the celadons being made at the same time in Chekiang province at the few surviving country celadon kilns. These latter glazes might be described as 'regressed' celadons and are higher in lime and lower in alkalis than the glazes used in the Sung dynasty.

Ground glass in chinese glazes

Those Chinese glazes that are exceptionally high in alkalis are often fluxed with ground glass rather than felspar. The most important examples of this type of glaze are the nineteenth-century Chinese copper-red glazes, analysed at Sèvres in the 1880s.[10] These analyses show the glazes to be unusual in many ways:

1. They are high in alkalis and very low in alumina, which is an impossible combination with felspathic glazes because felspars contain at least as much alumina as potash and soda.
2. They contain fair amounts of lead oxide, but most of this lead evaporates in the firing.
3. Strangest of all, they are low-silica glazes when placed in the kiln, but high-silica glazes when taken out.

This last phenomenon is due to the proportion of silica increasing relative to the fluxes, while three-quarters of the lead in the glaze vapourizes in the 1280°C firing. Below is an example of a Chinese copper-red glaze before and after firing, together with two more analyses of similar Chinese copper-red glazes in the fired state.

	SiO_2	Al_2O_3	Fe_2O_3	PbO	CuO	CaO	MgO	K_2O	Na_2O	$(K_2O + Na_2O)$
Chinese copper red (raw)[10]	62·83	4·35	0·86	12·9	0·63	7·57	1·69	5·94	2·91	(8·85)
Same glaze (fired) [10]	70·18	6·57	0·91	3·9	0·54	9·00	1·65	4·79	2·71	(7·5)
Copper red Chinese (Seger)[22]	71·07	3·24	1·4	4·15	0·92	9·2	1·75	8·11		(8·11)
Chinese copper red[10]	73·9	6·00	2·1	traces	4·6	7·3	traces	3·0	3·1	(6·1)

This last analysis, made in the 1850s, may be incorrect, because when a glaze is made up to these proportions it comes out of the kiln metallic and cindery from the presence of too much copper. It may be that most of the 4·6% allocated to copper is actually lead, for these two oxides were sometimes tested together in glaze analysis. Assuming 0·6% for the copper and 4·0% for the lead, this would bring the glaze nearer to the other two Chinese copper-red glazes; although, of course, this is only a guess at what might have happened.

If glazes are to be calculated from any of these analyses it would be best to work from the first *unfired* analysis. Ground glass (cullet) would be necessary in the recipe as this is a high-alkali, low-alumina material. In fact, it was actually the main material used to make these Chinese copper-reds.

4. *Phosphatic glazes*
The subject of the presence of phosphorous oxide in early Chinese glazes has been somewhat complicated by an article published in 1915[25] which describes the discovery by analysis of P_2O_5 percentages as high as 8·5% in

Sung glazes. (This is at least five times as much as any other researchers have found since.) The article claims that high phosphorous figures of this type are typical for most Sung glazes — including celadons — and even some Sung bodies were found to contain something like $2.4\%\,P_2O_5$. The full analyses of two Sung Chüns supplied in the 1915 article are as follows (together with a modern analysis of another Chün glaze):

	SiO_2	Al_2O_3	CaO	$(K_2O + Na_2O)$	Fe_2O_3	P_2O_5	CuO	MgO
'Hard blue' Chün Sung (1915)[25]	70.3	10.6	5.9	5.0	2.3	7.2	trace	
'Soft blue' Chün Sung (1915)[25]	68.2	9.5	7.1	5.9	2.5	8.0	trace	
Violet Chün Sung (1960s)[5]	72.8	9.94	8.8	4.57	1.58	0.5		1.5

The accuracy of the first two analyses is difficult to check because it is very hard to design a glaze that contains more phosphorous than lime (bone ash, the usual source of phosphorous contains more lime than phosphorous). However, one cannot help wondering if there might have been some fault in the analytical methods that produced these high phosphorous figures. Once again the relative scarcity of analyses of North Chinese glazes makes it difficult to say whether they are definitely right or wrong.

Leaving aside these rather controversial analyses we can say that phosphorous is usually found in Chün glazes from 0.5 to 1.5%. It has also been found in an analysis of a Kuan glaze at 0.5%, and it is believed to be present in Ju glazes in similar quantities. As far as we know its presence in Sung celadon glazes is usually well below these amounts.

Effect of phosphorous in glazes
The main effect of phosphorous in glazes is to encourage the formation of millions of bubbles, which, unlike those produced by alumina, cannot easily be cleared by longer firing or more heat. An increase in firing temperature causes the small bubbles to coalesce into larger bubbles, and the eventual bursting of the bubbles of gas at top temperatures leaves 'pinholes', or even quite large pits, in the fired surfaces of some phosphatic glazes. Phosphorous is also credited with producing a curious 'glass-in-glass' effect that can give an elusive (though sometimes very pronounced) blue tint to a glaze. These two effects do not always occur together: some Chüns can have this blue tone and yet be quite glassy, but in the best glazes the soft depth produced by the mass of bubbles is enhanced spectacularly by the blue 'Chün effect'. However, as anyone who has experimented with these phosphatic glazes knows, one is just as likely to get a rather dull, frothy-looking glaze with no trace of the 'Chün-blue' at all.

The milky-white or blue opalescence encouraged by phosphorous pentoxide in small amounts can also be produced by adding boric oxide (from colemanite), or lead oxide to a stoneware glaze. Analyses of some Chinese Chüns show the presence of a considerable amount of lead, but no phosphorous pentoxide and the famous *flambé* streaks in lead-containing Chinese copper-red glazes are similar to the opalescent streaks seen in some Chüns. The fact that boron (like phosphorous) is a glass-forming oxide of the same type as silica lends support to the theory — put forward by Steger (1951), [26] Sundius (1963),[5] and Cardew (1969)[1] — that the blue and milky-white colours in Chün glazes are optical effects produced by the non-mixing of two types of glass within the glaze.

Rival theories on the cause of this Chün-effect include: (1) fine, undissolved silica from plant ash (particularly grass or reed ash) in the glaze (Leach)[27] and (2) the presence of the blue mineral vivianite (ferrous phosphate) in the Chüns (Hetherington).[28] These different theories do not necessarily invalidate each other. In fact undissolved silica, particularly, does give something of this effect in thickly applied Chinese celadons. Good Chün glazes are some of the most difficult Chinese glazes to re-create, but the analyses of Chinese Chüns do at least enable us to make a start in the right areas of composition.

4. *Iron oxide in Chinese glazes*
Iron oxide provides the colour in virtually all early Chinese stoneware glazes, but the colours that iron will give are profoundly affected by small amounts of impurities in the glaze such as titanium dioxide (TiO_2), manganous oxide (MnO) and phosphorous pentoxide (P_2O_5). Because of these 'modifiers' the same amount of iron oxide in Chüns, celadons and Kuan glazes will give sky-blue, grass-green, and bluish-grey colours respectively, even though the base glazes are broadly the same and are fired under similar reducing conditions. Probably the most powerful of these 'modifiers' is titanium dioxide, and it is the effect of titanium on iron that helps to produce the range of colours from light-blue to olive-green that are characteristic of Chinese celadons. In fact, a slight variation in the titanium content of celadons seems to have as much influence on the blueness or greenness of the resulting glaze as slight differences in degrees of reduction. The amounts of titanium needed to change the natural bluish colour of reduced iron to the typical celadon-green are very small — more than 0·1% TiO_2 will make the glaze fire more green than blue.[24] Up to 1·7% TiO_2 has been found in Chinese celadons,[22] although this seems to be exceptional and the most usual amounts found in the celadons of the Sung dynasty are between 0·1 and 0·2%.

It is often said that the green colours of celadons represent a mixture of yellow (oxidized) and blue (reduced) oxides of iron. (Reduction is the chemical process deliberately produced in stoneware firings by cutting down the amount of air allowed for burning the fuel and producing those gases, such as carbon monoxide and hydrogen that 'reduce' iron oxide from a higher (Fe_2O_3) to a lower (FeO) oxide by 'stealing' some oxygen from the first state to create the second.) However, in practice, it is almost impossible to make a blue celadon fire green — or a green celadon fire blue. When, as sometimes happens, a blue celadon glazed article is (literally) half reduced and half oxidized, it does not show the gradual transition from yellow, through green, to blue, that the theory seems to demand. It seems more likely that the powerful yellowish tint of titanium combining with the blue of reduced iron is responsible for green celadons, and the (undeniable) difference in colour that degrees of reduction also produce are rather secondary to this effect.

High iron glazes

Chinese black glazes have come to be known as *temmokus* — the word 'temmoku' being used by the Japanese to describe the dark-glazed, South Chinese tea bowls made in Fukien province in the Sung dynasty. The word is used nowadays fairly broadly to describe Japanese, Chinese (and Western) high-fired glazes that are black or brown in colour and contain considerable iron oxide (about 4—10%).

Three main types of temmoku were made in Sung China — two in the South and one in the North — but unfortunately none of them seem to have been analysed quantitively, and so the following remarks are based more on general glaze experience than specific technical information. The first, and most familiar, of these temmoku glazes is that used on the Chien ware tea bowls made in Fukien province.

Chien ware

Chien ware bowls are glazed with a thick, lustrous and oily-black or black-brown glaze that runs downwards from the rims and collects in a thick roll somewhat short of the bare clay at the feet of the bowls (see Fig. 19). Where the glaze is left thinner on the rims it usually has a dull brown tone and, as these rims tend to be rough, they are often bound with metal, in the same way as Northern Ting wares. An attractive feature of these Chien glazes are the fine vertical streaks and flecks of brown within the black glazes, which give an overall impression of light and dark fur. In fact, these Chien glazes have been known from early times to the Chinese by the name 'hare's fur'.

The fine brown streaks in Chien glazes may be caused by an effect similar to that suggested for the *flambé* effects in Chün and copper-red glazes: namely, a non-mixing of two glasses within the glaze. A technical (but unfortunately not analytical) study of a Sung Chien glaze supports this 'glass in glass' idea by noting that: 'The outer glaze surface was streaked with streamers of brown and greenish black as if two immiscible coloured glasses had run down the sloping surface of the piece'.[29]

The boiling and bubbling of the maturing Chien glaze probably disturbs the lime-rich and iron-rich layers that such glazes tend to evolve during a firing, thus bringing concentrations of the iron-rich glass to the surface

Fig. 19 Chien ware tea bowl with metal-bound rim from Fukien province, South China (diameter about 5 inches). Sung dynasty. It is bowls like this that the Japanese call 'temmoku' and most examples in Japanese collections have their rims bound in metal to cover the slightly rough edge where the glaze has run thinner in the firing. The Chinese liken the finely streaked glaze to 'hare's fur'. Much of the character and richness of the glaze on Chien bowls is due to the influence of the iron-rich stoneware clay beneath the glaze. *Victoria and Albert Museum*

where they appear as browner marks or streaks running downwards within the fluid glaze. The whole process is a mixing (or non-mixing) of two different glasses.

Despite their obvious fluidity, it is possible that Chien glazes are higher than normal in alumina, and their tendency to run may be due to a low silica content, the $SiO_2 + Al_2O_3$ total being too low for the firing temperature used. Again this is a purely technical judgement. In reality, the Chien glaze is one of the finest used on Sung ceramics.

Chi-chou ware

The other Southern temmoku ware was made in Southern Kiangsi, not far from the market town of Chi-chou, and, like the Chien kilns, the main production was tea bowls.

The two types of Southern tea bowl are not easily confused, since the clays used for the Chi-chou bowls were light-coloured and the glazes looked dull and under-fired. This must have encouraged the Chi-chou potters to develop their highly original decorative techniques. Their techniques included such methods as cut paper resist, leaf resist, as well as a somewhat puzzling type of resist process that allowed a brown-black underglaze to show through, what seems to have been a variegated phosphatic overglaze, in finely detailed patterns of birds, insects, or geometrical motifs. The dullness of the glaze, the light body, the oxidized firings, and the use of phosphatic overglazes are all reminiscent of some of the earliest black-glazed stonewares made in North China during the T'ang dynasty.

Northern temmoku

Some of the finest pots ever made in China were produced in the Northern temmoku kilns of the eleventh and twelfth centuries. They were mostly made from fine, light-coloured stoneware clays and fired at temperatures rather higher than those generally used in the South and, apparently, in oxidizing to neutral atmospheres. The glazes often had a thick, dull, rich blackness and tended to show a light brown or straw-coloured transparency if the glaze was thin. Northern temmokus were often decorated with rusty splashes or brushed patterns of nearly pure iron oxide which contrasted well with the slightly dull black glazes beneath. The composition of these Northern temmokus is unknown at the moment, although they seem to have much in common with the Albany slip clays of America (for examples see Figs. 22, 20, 21).

Fig. 20 Honan dish with six-lobed rim and lightly indented sides (diameter 7·75 inches). Sung dynasty. Lustrous black glaze flecked with rusty specks. The non-vitrifying North Chinese clays allowed more extreme shapes than was possible with the Southern porcelains. *Sotheby and Co., London*

Fig. 21 North Chinese tea bowl, black glaze on buff stoneware (diameter 3 inches). 'Sung dynasty type'. The monumental character of this bowl belies its true size. This particular form, with its slightly inturned rim, was used at most Sung kilns, particularly those making Chün and celadon wares. *British Museum*

Fig. 22 Black-glazed, North Chinese bottle (height 10·5 inches). Sung dynasty. Almost pure iron oxide can be used to decorate black glazes of this type. If the pigment is used thinly it will fire to a good rust colour that brings the black glaze to life. This bottle has been fired high enough to bring out the best characteristics of both glaze and decoration. *British Museum*

Fig. 23 Stoneware teapot with calligraphic decoration (height 10 inches). Made by the Chinese potter Peter Lau (now working in Malaysia) while he was a student in England. It is a white porcelain glaze containing small amounts of bone ash and titanium dioxide with overglaze painting in black iron oxide and is reduction fired to about 1250°C. The design of the handle and lid is derived from Malaysian country pottery and the two main characters mean 'never empty'. Glaze recipe: potash felspar 35·5, flint 36·5, China clay 15, whiting 13·0, dolomite 4·0, rutile 0·5, bone ash 0·5.

6 Calculations by the Percentage Method

Most of the analyses of Far Eastern glazes in this book can be re-created with the usual pottery raw materials. The calculations used work directly with the analyses of the original glazes and with the analyses of the various raw materials obtainable from the suppliers of pottery materials. We use the *fired* analyses of the glazes and the *unfired* or raw analyses of the materials.

There are only a few main principles involved in calculation by the percentage method and an electronic pocket calculator speeds up the work considerably. The best type of calculator for this type of calculation is one with a memory and also the capacity to repeat one part of a sum as long as necessary — usually done by simply pressing the = key. Another advantage is a special 'percentage' key.

Most of the glaze calculation by the percentage method makes use of two simple calculation procedures. Once these are grasped, a large number of fine Chinese and Japanese glazes become accessible and the only limitations are how we decide to use them.

Problem 1.

If a glaze contains 12% CaO in its analysis, and whiting contains 56% CaO in its analysis, how much whiting will provide 12% CaO?

The accurate answer is found by dividing the amount of CaO in the whiting into the amount of CaO in the glaze analysis, then multiplying the result by 100:

> (12 divided by 56) x 100 = 21·43 parts of whiting
> 21·43 parts of whiting therefore gives 12% CaO

This is the main type of calculation using the percentage method, and it is repeated with every oxide in the glaze analysis until there are no more amounts of oxides still to be found and the recipe is complete.

Problem 2. explains how to deal with the other oxides brought into a glaze when a raw material containing more than one oxide in its analysis is used. These associated oxides all play their part in satisfying the glaze analysis and we need to know the exact amounts in which they have been introduced, so that we can then subtract them from the original glaze analysis, together with the main oxide found by the method shown above. The method involves 'percentages of percentages' and is rather simpler than it sounds.

Percentages of percentages
This type of calculation is best approached by understanding the close links between decimals and percentages; for instance, 0·5 of a number is the same as 50% of it; 0·25 the same as 25% of it; or 0·176 is the same as 17·6% of it. Therefore, if we need to know, say, 21·43% of 56 we *multiply* 56 by 0·2143, which gives the answer 12·0.

Armed with both methods of calculation we can solve the following problem:

Problem 2.

If a glaze needs 12% CaO, and wollastonite contains 47% CaO + 51% SiO$_2$, how much wollastonite will supply 12% CaO, and how much SiO$_2$ will be brought into the glaze with it?

The answers are found by *dividing* the CaO in wollastonite (47%) into the CaO needed in the glaze (12%) and multiplying the answer by 100:

$(12·0 \div 47) \times 100 = 25·53$ (parts of wollastonite needed in glaze)

To find how much silica is brought into the glaze by the 25·53 parts of wollastonite, *multiply* the amount of the silica in wollastonite (51%) by 0·2553 (we know this to be the same as 25·53% of 51% SiO$_2$):

$51·0 \times 0·2553 = 13\%$ SiO$_2$

These two calculations tell us that 25·53 parts of wollastonite will supply 12·0% of CaO and 13% of SiO$_2$ to a glaze.

(All this might seem complicated but a certain amount of practice with a calculator will show that it takes far longer to explain these calculations than it does to actually work them out.)

These two techniques are really all that are needed for most glaze calculations by the percentage method, the rest of the work being simple subtraction. The most valuable aspect of the technique is that the amounts of raw materials found by these calculations are the amounts used in the final glaze recipes. No molecular weights or molecular formulae are used at all — we are simply dealing with the real weights of the oxides in the glazes and the real weights of the oxides in the raw materials.

Order of oxides found in glaze calculation
By now the reader might be wondering how we make sure that we do not

52

go 'over the top' with the associated oxides when using a complex material. This is simply a matter of practice and an increasing familiarity with analyses of materials and glazes. The main safeguard against over-doing a particular oxide is the order that has been evolved for finding the oxides in a glaze. This order tends to bring the more complicated materials in first and usually ends with a simple 'topping up' of pure oxides such as flint (SiO_2) and iron oxide (Fe_2O_3).

The order that gives the greatest protection against overdoing any particular oxide is:

the alkalis, alumina, magnesia, phosphorous, lime, silica, and *iron*
$K_2O + Na_2O$ Al_2O_3 MgO P_2O_5 CaO SiO_2 Fe_2O_3

When actually working out a glaze we would start by finding the potash and soda — probably using felspar or Cornish stone — then find the remaining alumina with some type of clay. If there was magnesia in a glaze we might use dolomite or talc; the lime might come from whiting or wollastonite and, finally, any few per cent of silica or iron still to be found would be supplied by flint, or quartz and iron oxide.

Calculation of a glaze from a percentage analysis

Everything that has been explained so far can be seen as an actual example of glaze calculation by the percentage method. For example we might begin with the 1170°C silica-alumina-lime eutectic, using Treviscoe china clay, whiting and flint to make the glaze. The 1170° lime eutectic, and the materials used to make it have the following analyses:

	SiO_2	Al_2O_3	CaO	$(K_2O + Na_2O)$	Loss
1170°C silica-alumina-lime eutectic	62·0	14·75	23·5		
Treviscoe kaolin	48·3	36·9		2·6	11·11
whiting			56·0		44·0
flint	100				

As there are no alkalis in the glaze we begin with the alumina, *dividing* the amount of alumina in the clay into the amount needed in the glaze, then *multiplying* by 100: (14·75 ÷ 36·9) x 100 = 40·0. Therefore 40 parts of kaolin are needed in the glaze. We now make the mental adjustment that tells us that if we multiply all the other oxides in the kaolin analysis (see above) by 0·4 we will discover how much silica and alkalis have been brought into the glaze with the 14·75% Al_2O_3.

Silica in raw kaolin: 48·3 multiplied by 0·4 = 19·3% SiO_2
Alkalis in raw kaolin: 2·6 multiplied by 0·4 = 1·04% $(K_2O + Na_2O)$

We now know that 40 parts of kaolin has given us 19·3% SiO_2, 14·74% Al_2O_3 and 1·04% $K_2O + Na_2O$. All these oxides can now be subtracted from the glaze to discover what remains to be found:

	SiO_2	Al_2O_3	CaO	$(K_2O + Na_2O)$
glaze:	62·0	14·75	23·5	
kaolin 40 parts:	19·3	14·75		1·04
Still to be found:	42·7	X	23·5	

The next oxide on the list is lime. We divide the amount of lime (CaO) in whiting (56·0) into the amount needed in the glaze (23·5) and multiply the answer by 100: (23·5 ÷ 56) x 100 = 42 (parts of whiting). This takes care of the lime. All that remains is the 42·7% SiO_2 and this is easily provided by pure flint or quartz (42·7 parts). The recipe is therefore: kaolin 40, whiting 42, flint 42·7.

This recipe gives us the 1170°C silica-alumina-lime eutectic, although these are two things that need some explanation. Firstly, we have 1·0% too much $K_2O + Na_2O$. This is unavoidable as all clays contain some alkali and this 1·0% should make little difference to the glaze. Secondly, the recipe, although calculated from a percentage analysis, does not add up to 100. This does not matter as long as the relative proportions of the ingredients are correct (which they are). It is the result of using raw materials that have 'losses on ignition' — in this case 11·11% water from the clay and 44·0% CO_2 from the whiting. The important point is that the recipe provides 100% of oxides in the right proportions and of the right type to make the glaze. To bring the recipe to a percentage form all the ingredients should be added together (40 + 42 + 42·7 = 124·7) and then each individual quantity should be *divided* by this total, and multiplied by 100. This gives the true percentage recipe as follows:

kaolin   32·1
flint   34·2
whiting 33·7

Such a glaze is rather too high in clay to use on biscuit, but should work well on dry clay as a raw glaze. The firing temperature would have to be about 1200°C.

Although it has taken a fair amount of space to explain how to create this glaze there are few actual calculations involved and these are fairly simple. One more example of calculation by this type of percentage method should be enough to deal with most of the problems likely to be encountered.

Calculation of a typical Chinese glaze using the percentage method

The next calculation involves the re-creation of a Chinese Sung celadon using Cornish stone, wollastonite, Treviscoe kaolin, dolomite, flint and pure iron oxide to provide the oxides found by analysis to be present in the Chinese glaze. The procedures are the same as those used for the eutectic glaze, but as the Chinese glaze contains a greater variety of oxides, the process takes longer.

	SiO_2	Al_2O_3	Fe_2O_3	TiO_2	CaO	MgO	K_2O	Na_2O	$(K_2O + Na_2O)$
Sung celadon[8]	66·33	14·28	1·0	0·03	11·34	1·17	4·3	0·99	(5·29)
Raw Materials									
Cornish stone	72·04	15·62			2·21	0·18	4·39	3·98	(8·37)
wollastonite	51·0				47·0				
Treviscoe kaolin	48·3	36·9	0·75	0·04			2·5	0·1	(2·6)
dolomite					31·25	19·8			
pure(synthetic) iron oxide			100						
flint	100								

This Chinese glaze is a South Chinese Sung dynasty celadon of the finest type and shows the typical 2:1 balance of lime to alkalis, typical celadon silica and alumina figures, and a particularly low titanium figure that should allow a good blue tone from 1·0% iron oxide. Because of the very low TiO_2 figure, china clay rather than ball clay should be used in the 're-creation'. The use of wollastonite rather than whiting encourages a jade-like character from the glaze, and also allows the glaze to be reduced heavily in an oil-fired kiln without suffering too much from the effects of 'smoke-staining'.

The calculation uses the order of oxides previously described on page 53 (alkalis, alumina, magnesia, lime, silica, iron). The amount of each raw material needed is discovered by *dividing* the quantity of oxide found in that material *into* the quantity of the particular oxide needed in the glaze, and then multiplying the answer by 100. The associated oxides are found by the 'percentages of percentages' method, and after each material has been introduced, the oxides that it provides are subtracted from those still to be found, until there are no more oxides needed and the glaze is complete. Each new row (representing a new material) is underlined and subtracted from the row above it and the glaze can be double checked when complete by adding together all the underlined figures beneath the separate oxides. The totals should match the intended glaze. The completed glaze is as follows, and the recipe (which is usable as it stands) is on the left.

Blue Celadon (% by weight)	SiO$_2$ 66.33	Al$_2$O$_3$ 14.28	Fe$_2$O$_3$ 1.0	TiO$_2$ 0.03	CaO 11.34	MgO 1.17	(K$_2$O + Na$_2$O) 5.29
Cornish stone 63.2 parts To be found:	45.53 / 20.8	9.87 / 4.41	— / 1.0	— / 0.03	1.4 / 9.94	0.11 / 1.06	5.29 / X
Kaolin 11.9 parts To be found:	5.77 / 15.03	4.41 / X	— / 1.0	0.005 / 0.025	9.94	1.06	0.3 / X
Dolomite 5.33 parts To be found:	15.03		1.0	0.025	1.66 / 8.28	1.06 / X	
Wollastonite 17.6 parts To be found:	8.98 / 6.05		1.0	0.025	8.28 / X		
Flint 6.05 parts: To be found:	6.05 / X		1.0				
Red iron oxide 1.0 part To be found:			1.0 / X	0.025			
Total of under-lined oxides	66.33	14.28	1.0	0.005	11.34	1.17	5.59

The only discrepancies are that there is too little titanium (the amounts involved are too low to be important, even for titanium), and 0.3% too much alkali, but this too is of marginal importance. However, where clays that are particularly high in alkalis are used, an even more accurate method of percentage calculation can be employed that allows for this (described on pages 57—59).

It is taken for granted that the introduction of each new raw material is followed by the subtraction of the oxides that it provides from the 'to be found' line above. The stages that have been used in creating this glaze are:

1. Divide the K$_2$O + Na$_2$O (potash + soda) in the Cornish stone into the K$_2$O + Na$_2$O in the celadon, then multiply by 100 to give 63.2 (parts of Cornish stone). Multiply all the oxides in 100% Cornish stone by 0.632. *Subtract from line above.*

2. Divide all the Al$_2$O$_3$ in the kaolin into the Al$_2$O$_3$ still to be found, then multiply by 100 to give 11.9 (parts of kaolin). Multiply all the oxides in 100% kaolin by 0.119. *Subtract from line above.*

3. Divide all the MgO in the dolomite into the amount of MgO still to be found, then multiply by 100. Multiply the oxides in dolomite by 0.053. *Subtract from line above.*

4. Divide the CaO in wollastonite into the CaO still to be found, then

multiply by 100. Multiply all the oxides in wollastonite by 0·176. *Subtract from line above.*

5. Supply the remaining SiO_2 with pure flint (6·05 parts). *Subtract from line above.*

6. Supply the remaining iron with pure iron oxide (1·0 part). *Subtract from line above.* This is the last oxide needed and the glaze is now complete.

7. Add all underlined oxides together to check glaze. It should match the top line almost exactly.

Using a calculator

You will notice when doing the above calculations with a calculator how useful the 'repeat' capacity of a calculator can be. After the first oxide in a material has been multiplied by, say, 0·25 (to find 25% of the amount of it in a material), each successive oxide can be multiplied by 0·25 simply by pressing out the quantity found in the material analysis and pressing the '=' key for the answer. Should the calculator have a % key, you do not even have to make the 25% = x0·25 mental adjustment, instead you simply press out 'quantity of oxide' x 25% to get the answer. For every other oxide in the material you merely press out the quantity it appears in the material's analysis and press the % key for the answer.

Simultaneous calculation
The kind of calculation just described will be suitable for nine out of ten glazes, but should two materials be needed in the glaze that *both* contain appreciable amounts of alkalis and alumina, some method must be devised to discover the *one* combination of the two materials that fits the demands of the intended glaze. Say, for instance, that we wish to use a red earthenware clay with Cornish stone to make a temmoku glaze based on Albany slip. We find that we have the following analyses for Albany slip, the Cornish stone and the red clay:

	SiO_2	Al_2O_3	Fe_2O_3	TiO_2	CaO	MgO	$(K_2O + Na_2O)$
Albany slip	62·75	16·67	5·53	0·77	6·48	3·25	4·38 (average)[30, 31]
Cornish stone	72·04	15·62			2·01	0·18	8·37
Fremington clay	52·66	18·17	6·22	1·02	4·69	3·42	3·68[1]

(It should be noticed that the analysis of Albany slip is in the fired state while the stone and clay analyses are of the 'raw' and unfired materials.)

To find the one combination of Cornish stone and Fremington clay that will give the 16·67 Al_2O_3 and the 4·38 $(K_2O + Na_2O)$ we set out the problem as a simultaneous equation, with the amount of stone needed being 'A' and the amount of clay 'B':

Equation (1) A × (alumina in stone) + (alumina in clay) × B
= alumina in glaze.

Equation (2) A × (alkalis in stone) + (alkalis in clay) × B = alkalis in glaze
In numerical terms the two equations are as follows:

Equation (1) $15.62A + 18.17B = 16.67$

Equation (2) $8.37A + 3.68B = 4.38$

To solve the equations we divide all the numbers in equation (1) by 15·62, and all the numbers in equation (2) by 8·37:

Equation (1) now becomes: $A + 1.16B = 1.06$

Equation (2) now becomes: $A + 0.44B = 0.52$

We can now eliminate 'A' by subtracting (2) from (1) to give: $0.72B = 0.54$. It is now easy to find 'B' for it must be 0·54 divided by 0·72, which is: 0·75. We already know that when an oxide is multiplied by 0·75 it means that the actual amount of the raw material needed in the recipe is 75%, so with 'B' representing the clay we know that the recipe needs 75 parts of clay. Now that we know the value of 'B' we can substitute the value just found for 'B' in any of the equations to find 'A'. For instance, equation (1) in its second stage now becomes: $A + (1.16 \times 0.75) = 1.06$, which becomes $A + 0.87 = 1.06$, so by subtracting 0·87 from 1·06 we can find 'A' which equals: 0·19. We now know that the recipe needs 19 parts of Cornish stone and have established the two most important ingredients in the imitation Albany slip recipe: 75 parts Fremington clay, 19 parts Cornish stone.

These two materials are now put into a table and any other oxides still needed for the glaze are calculated in the manner already demonstrated.

	SiO_2	Al_2O_3	Fe_2O_3	TiO_2	CaO	MgO	$(K_2O + Na_2O)$
Albany slip:	62·75	16·67	5·53	0·77	6·48	3·25	4·38
Fremington clay 75 parts	<u>39·5</u>	13·62	<u>4·66</u>	0·76	3·5	2·56	<u>2·76</u>
To be found:	23·25	3·05	0·87	X	2·98	0·69	1·62
Cornish stone 19 parts	<u>13·68</u>	2·96			0·38		1·59
To be found:	9·57	X	0·87		2·6	0·69	X
Dolomite 3·4 parts					1·6	0·69	
To be found:	9·57		0·87		1·0	X	
Whiting 1·8 parts					1·0		
To be found:	9·57		0·87		X		
Flint 9·57 parts	<u>9·57</u>						
To be found:	X		0·87				
Red iron 0·9 parts			0·9				
(glaze complete)			X				
Total of underlined oxides:	62·75	16·58	5·56	0·76	6·48	3·25	4·35

We can see from this that the simultaneous equations have worked well, if not quite to the hundredth part of the oxides. This glaze is obviously a raw glaze like the original Albany slip. The high magnesia content of this glaze (3·25%) makes it much glossier if fired above cone eight (1250°C).

Using two materials at once in a glaze requires a certain confidence that the resulting simultaneous blend will not go 'over the top' in such oxides as silica and iron, but this is only a matter of practice and experience. Eventually one comes to recognize which raw materials are most suited for which glazes, for instance, low-alumina clays are particularly useful for designing raw glazes that need a high clay content in the glaze, as they allow this without providing too much alumina.

The last two types of calculation, employing the percentage method, are used to bring any glaze recipe (where analyses of the materials used are known) and any 'Seger formula' published for a glaze, into percentage form. Thus, if we want to understand a glaze better, or copy it with different materials, we must know how to express that glaze in percentage form.

From a glaze recipe to a percentage analysis

The technique used for this is simply the 'percentages of percentages' method already explained. For instance one of the most famous stoneware and porcelain glazes used for many years in Stoke-on-Trent has the recipe 85 Cornish stone, 15 whiting.[32] Why is this such a successful glaze? The first step to understanding the answer is to find the analyses of Cornish stone and whiting.

	SiO_2	Al_2O_3	Fe_2O_3	MgO	CaO	K_2O	Na_2O	Loss
Purple Cornish stone:[32]	72·1	15·96	0·24	0·13	2·54	3·34	2·6	1·96
Whiting:					56·0			44·0

To find 85% of all the oxides in Cornish stone we multiply each one by 0·85. To find how much CaO is provided by 15% of whiting we multiply 56 by 0·15:

	SiO_2	Al_2O_3	Fe_2O_3	MgO	CaO	K_2O	Na_2O	$(K_2O + Na_2O)$
85 Purple stone:	61·285	13·56	0·2	0·11	2·16	2·84	2·21	(5·05)
15 Whiting:					8·4			
Total of oxides:	61·285	13·56	0·2	0·11	10·56	2·84	2·21	(5·05)

Because of the losses associated with both the Cornish stone and the whiting, the total of oxides is only 90·76. To bring them to the hundred per cent that will make it possible to compare this glaze with other porcelain glazes, we *divide* each oxide in the total by 90·76, then *multiply* by 100. (*If your calculator has a % key, still divide the first oxide (silica) by 90·76,* but press the % key for the answer. For each successive oxide after this merely press out the quantity of that oxide found in the 'total of oxides' above and press the % key for the answer. This will give the amount of that oxide found in the percentage analysis of the glaze.)

	SiO_2	Al_2O_3	Fe_2O_3	MgO	CaO	$(K_2O + Na_2O)$
85/15 glaze: (%)	67·52	14·94	0·22	0·12	11·63	5·56 (99·99%)

We see at once from this that the '85/15' recipe is yet another example of the 'ideal' type of oriental porcelain and celadon glaze, with all that this implies in terms of quality of surface and long maturing range. Its best temperature is probably cone 8—9.

Seger formula to percentage analysis

The final problem in this chapter on calculation concerns glazes that are expressed in the Seger formula style and which we would like to change into the percentage form. The technique for changing a Seger formula for a glaze into a percentage analysis is as follows:

1. Put all the oxides into the order preferred for the percentage method that is: SiO_2, Al_2O_3, Fe_2O_3, TiO_2, CaO, MgO, K_2O, Na_2O, P_2O_5, MnO.

2. Multiply each oxide by its molecular weight — this brings all the oxides in the list to their real weights.

3. Although the list is now in terms of real weights they still need to become *percentage weights*. This is achieved by adding all the real weights together, dividing the total into that found for each oxide in 2. and then multiplying the result by 100. (When using a calculator *divide* the total into the first oxide on the list (say, silica) and press the % key for the answer. To bring each oxide after this to its percentage state simply press out the total found for it in 2. and press the % key for the answer.)

A practical example of the procedure might arise as follows:

Seger cones as glazes

We might read in a book the interesting fact that Seger cones make first-class *glazes* at about 100°C higher than the temperatures they are designed to indicate.[33] This is particularly true of Seger cone 4, the composition of which is often used in the West for making porcelain glazes, for the temperature range 1230°—1300°C. Much of the literature concerning both Chinese and Western glazes makes the point that the 'cone 4 type of white-ware glaze' has a composition and appearance similar to the best Chinese glazes.[34] Why is this? Well, the answer should be found by turning the Seger formula for cone 4 into a percentage analysis, then comparing this analysis with the glazes we have already studied. The first step is to find the 'formula' for Seger cone 4:

$$\text{Seger cone 4:[22]} \quad \begin{array}{l} 0 \cdot 3 \ K_2O \\ \\ 0 \cdot 7 \ CaO \end{array} \quad 0 \cdot 5 \ Al_2O_3 \quad 4 \cdot 0 \ SiO_2$$

The three steps for changing a 'formula' into a percentage analysis are now taken:

(1)	(Mol. Wts)	(2)	(3)	
SiO_2 4·0 x	60·1	= 240·4	All oxides are	SiO_2 67·0
Al_2O_3 0·5 x	101·9	= 50·95	now *divided* by 358·88	Al_2O_3 14·2
K_2O 0·3 x	94·2	= 28·26	then *multiplied* by 100	K_2O 7·8
CaO 0·7 x	56·1	= 39·27		CaO 11·0

Total of real weights: 358·88

The percentage analysis of Seger cone 4 is therefore:

SiO_2 67, Al_2O_3 14·2, CaO 11·0, K_2O 7·8

At first sight this glaze appears to be exactly the 'ideal' or 'lime-alkali' celadon-Chün-porcelain glaze that has been mentioned so often already. However, a second look at this analysis shows it to be considerably higher in alkalis (at 7·8%) than most of the celadons and porcelain glazes so far discussed. It is actually moving from the 'lime-alkali' class to the 'felspathic' class as its theoretical recipe suggests:

felspar 41·5, flint 27·5, kaolin 13·0, whiting 18·0 ('Seger cone 4' glaze)

It is worth adding, as a conclusion to this chapter on calculation, that glazes created by the percentage method very rarely need any adjustments to bring them nearer to the desired qualities — as long as the analyses of materials are reliable and the original glaze analyses are accurate. (Those glaze analyses that seem suspect in this book have been pointed out as such.) Any problems with glazes made by this method tend to be physical rather than chemical — for instance, too much clay in a recipe makes a glaze crawl although its quality is otherwise good. Some materials too might need extra grinding (calcined clays, local clays and, often, dolomite), but after a certain amount of practice it should be possible to create glazes similar to those described in the next chapter.

7 Glaze Recipes

The glazes in this chapter have been arrived at by the methods of calculation described in chapter 6. They are mainly based on analyses of genuine Chinese glazes and have given good results even when the firing conditions have been less than perfect. Some of them have been designed to be used on both biscuited and raw, dry ware, while others have been specifically designed for use only on 'leather-hard' or biscuited pots.

Although this book is not primarily a recipe book, these few glazes illustrate many practical points that arise when theory is turned into practice. At the same time, however, they should turn out to be very satisfactory glazes in their own right.

Glaze 1. Porcelain glaze, 1240—1290°C, oxidation or reduction (see Fig. 24).

Potash felspar	25									
Wollastonite	27					ultimate analysis:				
China clay	12·5	SiO_2	Al_2O_3	Fe_2O_3	TiO_2	CaO	MgO	K_2O	Na_2O	$(K_2O + Na_2O)$
BKS (H) ball clay	12·5	69·04	11·49	0·5	0·24	13·18	1·16	3·7	0·64	(4·37)
Flint	20·0									
Talc	3·0									

This glaze is of the type that is suitable for raw-glazing unfired, dry pots, as well as those that have already been biscuit-fired. On suitable bodies it gives results that are very close to real Chinese porcelain glazes, particularly those glazes that were used on the less refined (but more interesting) blue and white porcelains, such as ginger jars and plates, painted with landscape patterns that were turned out by the million at Ching-tê Chên in the nineteenth century. Much of the character of this glaze is due to the use of wollastonite rather than whiting in the recipe, and the presence of a small amount of ball clay provides the small trace of iron that also gives life to the genuine Chinese porcelain clays and glazes.

The small amount of MgO provided by the talc improves the lustre and richness of the glaze above about 1250°C. It is very important that the ball clay used in the recipe is of the high-silica type (see analysis of BKS). If an

Fig. 24 Lidded jar with cobalt decoration by the author (height 8·5 inches, width 5·5 inches). Raw-glazed porcellanous stoneware, oxidized firing at about 1240°C. The jar was raw-glazed when quite dry, the inside of the lid and the jar being glazed first, allowed to dry out again, and then glazed outside by pushing the jar down into the glaze the right way up until the glaze reached the rim, lifting it out and immediately wiping the excess glaze from the foot. The decoration was painted on top of the dry glaze, using the recipe for cobalt pigment in Bernard Leach's *A Potter's Book*, namely: black cobalt oxide 20, manganese oxide 40, black iron oxide 30 and red clay 10. The porcelain glaze is Glaze No. 1 and can be used both on biscuit and raw, dry clay.

ordinary aluminous ball clay has to be substituted for this clay, about 6% clay and 6% quartz or flint should be used instead. This glaze has a lime percentage slightly higher than that typical of celadons, and the slight dullness produced when more than about 12% CaO is used in a glaze in the lower temperature range can be prevented by following the Chinese practice of cooling the kiln fairly quickly from its finishing temperature to about 1000°C. This lessens the tendency of the lime to crystallize and does not harm the ware as long as the kiln is clammed-up and allowed to cool at its own speed once 1000°C is reached.

This porcelain glaze ranges in character from a fine opaque white at 1230°C to a glossy, transparent, faintly bluish glaze at just below 1300°C. This particular recipe allows the glaze to be applied fairly heavily and one of its best qualities is seen when it has been thickly applied and fired in reduction to about 1250°C.

Glaze 2. Blue-green celadon, 1240—1280°C in good reduction.

Potash felspar	30·5								
Wollastonite	22·5	ultimate analysis:							
Flint or quartz	16·0	SiO_2	Al_2O_3	Fe_2O_3	TiO_2	CaO	MgO	K_2O	Na_2O
Talc	3·0	67·9	13·76	1·03	0·25	11·04	1·16	4·6	0·78
BKS (H) ball clay	12·5								
Kaolin or china clay	15·5			$(K_2O + Na_2O = 5·38)$					
Red iron oxide (synthetic)	0·5								
(from Wengers Ltd)									

This recipe gives a good blue-green celadon of fine surface quality and fresh colour and has been designed to be used on dry, raw clay, as well as on biscuit (see Fig. 17). It looks its best when applied thickly and fired just below 1250°C in fairly heavy reduction. It can be re-oxidized at top heat without losing its colour and this high temperature re-oxidation will give a good warm colour to the clays if they are of the right type. If the glaze is cooled fast to 1000°C it is more likely to show that 'fat' or 'waxy' quality where opacity is balanced by a soft surface glossiness, and the small amount of magnesia from the talc in the recipe reinforces the effect.

The blue-green celadon is at its best when used on porcelain, or the special 'grey porcelain' bodies made from siliceous ball clays and nepheline syenite and described at the end of the chapter. As might be expected from its analysis this recipe will also make an excellent porcelain glaze if the 0·5% iron oxide is left out. This 'synthetic' red iron oxide is of a particularly pure and fine type, and is useful in recipes where the exact amount of iron is important. Some of the cheaper grades of iron oxide seem to vary in strength (they probably contain some silica or clay) and this makes it difficult to gauge exactly how much iron to use. As the 'synthetic' iron is rather expensive, the cheaper grades can be used in high-iron glazes, such as temmokus and kakis where it is not quite so crucial to use an exact amount of iron. It will be noticed that while only 0.5% iron oxide is used in the recipe there is over 1.0% iron in the fired glaze. This is because some iron is also present in the other raw materials.

Glaze 3. 'Northern' celadon, 1230—1260°C, in good reduction.

Cornish stone	56.0							
Wollastonite	20.0				ultimate analysis:			
BKS (H) ball clay	10.0	SiO_2	Al_2O_3	Fe_2O_3	TiO_2	CaO	MgO	$(K_2O + Na_2O)$
EOBB/Y ball clay	10.0	67.2	13.8	1.77	0.26	10.85	1.15	4.83
Talc	3.5							
Red iron oxide (synthetic)	1.5							

This is a fine, dark olive-green glaze, which is rather glassy, and, like the genuine Chinese Northern celadons, reveals carving, engraving and combing in the clay with great clarity. Its maturing temperature is slightly lower than the blue-green celadon and it shows its best character between about 1230° and 1250°C. The remarks about firing and cooling for Glaze 2. also apply to this glaze. This too can be applied to both dry and biscuited clay. Celadons are, of course, classic reduction glazes, but the types that are highest in iron also show most attractive straw-yellow and amber colours in oxidation.

Glaze 4. Temmoku, 1260—1300°C Oxidized — 'Northern' temmoku. Reduced — 'Hare's fur' temmoku.

Cornish stone	42.5									
BBV ball clay	15.0				ultimate analysis:					
Molochite (dust)	13.0*	SiO_2	Al_2O_3	Fe_2O_3	TiO_2	CaO	MgO	K_2O	Na_2O	$(K_2O + Na_2O)$
Dolomite	15.5	62.6	16.55	5.55	0.8	6.45	3.52	2.6	1.96	(4.46)
Flint or quartz	7.0	(Calculated from the average of about five samples of Albany slip clays)								
Red iron oxide	4.5									
Rutile	0.5									

Although this glaze was created in an attempt to imitate a typical Northern or Honan temmoku, somewhat surprisingly, in a 1280°C reduction firing it produced a fine 'hare's fur' temmoku of the South Chinese or Chien type. The glaze also showed the Chien glaze's tendency to run thinly from the rim of the pot and collect in a roll at the limit of the dipping. This result makes one wonder whether the North and South Chinese temmokus might be closer to one another in analysis than the appearance of the glazes suggests, for, in oxidizing to neutral firings, this glaze shows many similarities to the plainer Northern black glazes. It also shows a typical 'Chinese' reaction to pure iron oxide painted thinly on top of the glaze in that it runs and merges with the glaze in the same flame-like manner as on authentic

* Molochite is a calcined china clay from English China Clays Ltd. The finest dust grade should be used, but if this is unavailable, 15% raw china clay can be substituted. The calcined clay has been used to lessen the risk of crawling when the glaze is thickly applied.

Chinese examples. Thinly applied and on light-coloured bodies, this glaze also shows the typical tendency of Northern temmokus to fire a transparent yellowish-brown rather like varnish, and again, this is characteristic of oxidized firings. Where the glaze is especially thin, (for instance, on sharp edges) it is almost white, which is rather surprising as the same glaze is quite black when thick. Some clues to this are found in Dr Sundius's microscopic work with cross-sections of Northern temmokus, which shows them to be made up of three distinct layers within the glaze: a white layer of lime-felspar crystals next to the clay, then a thicker layer of dark iron crystals, and, finally, a layer of transparent glass.[5] It may be that the layer of iron crystals can only form if the glaze is thick enough, and this would explain the very noticeable differences in glazes of this type. (Felspathic temmokus are quite different and show the famous 'black breaking to rust' effect when used thinly.)

The 'hare's fur' reaction

Because the 'hare's fur' effect seems to be encouraged by the boiling and bubbling of the glaze as it melts, it is probably better, in this case, to use carbonates, such as dolomite and whiting in temmoku recipes rather than their less reactive equivalents — wollastonite and talc. If the firing temperature has not been high enough to bring the magnesia in the glaze into the reaction, the resulting glaze is a dull, brown colour with a matt surface. The quality of the glaze changes very abruptly at the right temperature (apparently about $1260°C$), for it happens occasionally that a pot is taken from the kiln with one side showing a fine glossy black glaze, while the other side is still changing from the dull state.

As this glaze has a tendency to run slightly if thickly applied and the firing is high enough, it should not be taken too near to the foot of the pot in the glazing. A firing temperature between about 1280 and $1300°C$ seems to give the best results.

Glaze 5. Raw 'Albany slip', $1260-1300°C$, oxidation or reduction.

BBV ball clay 70
Potash felspar 20

ultimate analysis:

	SiO_2	Al_2O_3	Fe_2O_3	TiO_2	CaO	MgO	K_2O	Na_2O	$(K_2O + Na_2O)$
Dolomite 17									
Red iron oxide 5	62·1	16·8	5·65	0·95	6·34	3·59	3·8	0·67	(4·48)
Wollastonite 2									

In reduction, at the temperatures suggested, this recipe gives a fine smooth, glossy glaze with a dark bronze colour and with something of this metal's natural variety of tone and lustre. The glaze is very reminiscent of the famous 'dead leaf' glaze used on Chinese porcelain from the Sung dynasty to the present day, and it is on porcelain and porcellanous bodies that this glaze is seen at its best.

This is a raw glaze of the type that can be applied to pots that are still

Fig. 25 Teapot with mirror-black glaze and porcellanous stoneware body by the author (height 7·5 inches, overall width 9·5 inches). Neutral firing to about 1230°C. Mirror-black glazes were mainly used in the Southern porcelain factories from the eighteenth century onwards, but they are occasionally seen on the very rare 'Black Ting' ware of the Sung dynasty. Although this recipe contains about 0·5% cobalt oxide it is essentially a brown-black, rather than a blue-black colour, with the high manganese content 'overpowering' the cobalt. (Glaze No. 6).

shrinking after being made, i.e. the 'leather-hard' state. The glaze can also be used on raw, dry pots, and even on biscuited pots if it is not used too thickly. It is actually best used rather thinly for it seems to have remarkable 'covering power' and shows its best character as a thin coat on a fine clay.

The same remarks about the dangers of dullness from under-firing also apply to this raw 'Albany slip', which is definitely at its best in reduction. The stronger the reduction the more opaque, lustrous and rich in tone the glaze will appear. In oxidation when applied thinly, it will show the same brownish semi-transparency as Glaze 4.

Glaze 6. Mirror-black glaze, 1220—1250°C oxidation or reduction.

Flint or quartz	20·5									
Wollastonite	18·5	ultimate analysis:								
Potash felspar	19·0									
Kaolin (raw)	14·75	SiO_2	Al_2O_3	Fe_2O_3	CaO	MgO	$K_2O + Na_2O$	MnO	CoO	TiO_2
BKS (H) ball clay	14·75	63·31	11·5	9·5	9·12	0·1	3·3	2·4	0·47	0·2
Iron oxide	9·0									
Manganese dioxide	3·25									
Cobalt oxide	0·45									

This type of glaze became popular in China in the early eighteenth century, but glazes with a mirror-black appearance were in use in North China as early as the Sung dynasty. This particular glaze was reconstructed from an analysis of a Chinese glaze[10] used in the nineteenth century when it was usually fired in the cooler parts of the porcelain kilns near to the chimney, where the temperature was lower and the strong reducing atmosphere close to the fire mouth gave way to an atmosphere that was mainly oxidizing to neutral. The Chinese recipes for mirror-blacks made use of second-grade cobalt pigment, which is really a manganese ore containing a small amount of cobalt as a natural impurity — hence the unusually large amount of MnO_2 in the recipe. The high percentage of iron comes partly from this ore (which also contains iron), and partly from the red-firing clay that was another ingredient in the Chinese recipe.

The re-constructed recipe gives a fine mirror-black from 1220°C upwards in both oxidizing and reducing atmospheres, but has a tendency to run if fired higher than about 1250°C (see Fig. 25). The glaze is at its best when applied with medium thickness, but if it used thinly on a light body it can vary from golden-brown to black in a manner reminiscent of tortoise-shell — an attractive effect in its own right. If it is used too thickly it tends to become dull and crystalline and is not so satisfactory. The clay proportion in this glaze (equal parts of china clay and a siliceous ball clay) has been used because this quantity and mixture of clay has been found to give good results in dipping. It also prevents settling and solidifying of the glaze when not in use, and allows raw glazing on dry ware without the flaking and crawling that results from using glazes low in clay.

Glaze 7. Chinese blue stoneware glaze, 1250—1310°C, best fired in reduction, but can be used in oxidation too.

Potash felspar	30·5								
Wollastonite	15·0			ultimate analysis:[10]					
Flint or quartz	20·0								
BKS(H) ball clay	12·5	SiO_2	Al_2O_3	Fe_2O_3	TiO_2	CaO	MnO	CoO	$K_2O + Na_2O$
China clay	15·5	69·07	14·2	0·73	0·24	7·6	1·6	0·43	5·52
Red iron oxide (syn)	0·5								
Cobalt oxide	0·4								
Manganese dioxide	1·5								

This glaze is included because it is difficult to make a stoneware glaze coloured with cobalt that is not too garish and the good blue tone that this glaze has is the result of the original glaze being coloured with impure Chinese cobalt (a natural mixture of iron, manganese and cobalt oxides). This mixture is reproduced in the above recipe. The colour of this glaze (a medium blue) can be changed to a darker and richer blue by increasing the iron oxide in the recipe to 1·0%. The fact that this glaze is a typical celadon type, but coloured with small amounts of manganese and cobalt, as well as the usual iron oxide, enhances its good qualities.

Once again the clay content allows the glaze to be applied both to biscuit and dry clay, and it should be applied thickly (if it is thin the colour can look somewhat 'washed out'). The hotter the glaze is fired (within the limits suggested) the better it looks and good reduction gives the best results — since the green tone from the reduced iron is an important component of the glaze's colour.

The disadvantage of using glazes coloured with cobalt oxide is that they need to be ball-milled thoroughly to disperse the blue colour, which will otherwise appear as definite flecks in the finished glaze. Also great care must be taken to wash out very thoroughly the ball mill, pebbles and any sieves that might have been used, or every subsequent glaze mixed will show blue flecks after firing. If no ball mill is available it is probably better to use both cobalt carbonate and manganese carbonate (instead of the oxides) for they are much finer and mix more easily in the glaze batch.

Glaze 8. 'Mashiko Kaki', 1240° to 1310°C, oxidation or reduction.

Cornish stone	54·5	ultimate analysis:								
BKS (H) ball clay	10·0									
Kalbrite 2K	12·5	SiO_2	Al_2O_3	Fe_2O_3	TiO_2	CaO	MgO	K_2O	Na_2O	$(K_2O + Na_2O)$
Flint or quartz	9·0	68·4	14·3	6·54	0·36	3·7	2·0	2·3	2·25	(4·55)
Wollastonite	5·5									
Talc	6·0									
Red iron oxide	6·0									

This is a traditional Japanese (rather than a Chinese) glaze but it has been included because it is so exceptionally versatile, both as a highly attractive over-glaze and also as a basis for making good temmokus. It is a glaze that has been used to great effect by the famous potters, Bernard Leach and Shoji Hamada, particularly as an over-glaze and in combination with various methods of resist.

A good Kaki glaze used over another (usually more fluid) glaze gives a fascinating variety and richness of colour and texture, within the range of natural colours and tones typical of stoneware glazes, that cannot be obtained by other methods. The above glaze seems to show all the best characteristics of the Japanese original.[16]

By itself the Kaki glaze is a smooth rusty-brown glaze with a slight gloss, but it is at its best when used over slightly more fluid glazes such as celadons, temmokus or porcelain glazes. The extra flux supplied by the under-glazes seems to bring the Kaki glaze to life, making it appear a rich foxy-red colour where it is thick, dissolving into a brown-black, dusted with rust, where it is thinner. When thinner still, and used over a porcelain glaze, it looks like a greenish-brown celadon, but a celadon that transforms itself into a Kaki glaze wherever (by accident or design) it is applied more thickly. Thus, the

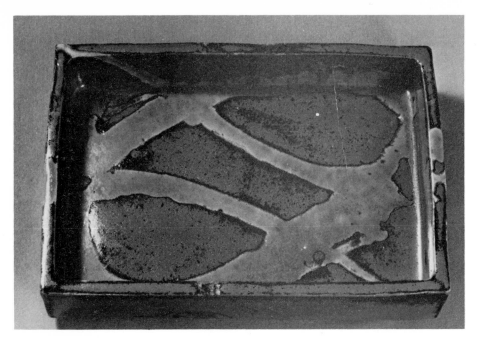

Fig. 26 Rectangular stone ware dish by Shoji Hamada (15 inches x 10 inches). Oxidized copper-green felspathic glaze, trailed with hot wax then re-dipped in Mashiko Kaki glaze giving a rust on green contrast. The underglaze used for this dish is a typical Japanese felspathic glaze made by adding small amounts of ash to felspar and is of a type hardly ever used on Chinese stoneware. The Kaki glaze is made by crushing a local building stone. Mashiko stone is a most versatile material giving excellent results as an overglaze and it makes good black temmokus with the addition of about 10 per cent wood ash.

Fig. 27 Large dish by the author (diameter 12 inches). Reconstructed Mashiko Kaki glaze (Glaze No. 8) over porcelain glaze (Glaze No. 1), reduction fired at about 1250°C.
This was first glazed overall with the porcelain glaze, then, before the glaze had completely dried, the diamond shapes (cut from newspaper and soaked in water) were laid on the surface of the glaze. It was then re-dipped in the Kaki glaze while still slightly damp and the paper-resist shapes were removed when the top glaze was nearly dry.

Fig. 28 Oval baking dish by the author. Kaki dip on rim and trailed Kaki decoration over dark-olive celadon (Glaze No. 8 over 3). Overall length 13 inches. Dishes of this shape are best made in two parts: the walls are thrown without a base, allowed to stiffen slightly then cut from the bat and lifted on to a prepared oval base (a slab of clay). Once the dish has stiffened sufficiently, excess clay can be cut away and the whole dish finished by slow turning on a kick-wheel. It is reduction fired in an oil-fired kiln at about 1240°C and the body is made from a mixture of ball-milled fireclay and ball clay powder.

one over-glaze can produce colours ranging from green, through dark-brown to rust simply by thickness. When these natural variations are combined with some form of resist (wax, paper, or even leaves) the possibilities are even greater (see Fig. 26).

The Kaki glaze is also exceptionally useful for trailing over other glazes, rather in the manner of slipware, and looks well over the darker, olive, celadons (Fig. 28), porcelain glazes and temmokus. It can also be used (with some discretion) over the blue glaze, although one of the best results comes from reversing this arrangement and trailing the blue glaze over the Kaki (itself used to cover another glaze).

Because the Mashiko glaze is originally prepared from a crushed rock, the above recipe has been designed with only enough clay to prevent it settling; the remainder of the clay being supplied by the 'Kalbrite 2K' which is a calcined high-alumina ball clay supplied by Watts, Blake, Bearne and Co. As this material is slightly coarser than most glaze materials the glaze benefits from ball milling.

Used as a basis for temmokus, the Kaki glaze gives a most interesting series of glazes with additions of ordinary wood-ash from about 1—15%. Those glazes lowest in ash will soon change to fine glossy-black temmokus, and eventually to clear, glassy amber or green glazes with increasing ash. These latter glazes are often seen on Japanese country pottery.

Fig. 29 One gallon stoneware teapot by the author (overall dimensions, including handle, 12 inches x 12 inches). The body of the pot was indented in three places while still on the wheel. The glaze is a slightly underfired felspathic temmoku with two bands of red iron on the glaze. The temmoku is Glaze No. 9 (reduction fired at 1250°C).

A particularly effective use of the Kaki glaze is had by trailing it on top of one of the Kaki/ash temmokus, a technique often used by Shoji Hamada.

Glaze 9. Felspathic temmoku. 1250—1310°C, oxidation or reduction (Fig. 29).

Potash felspar	55
London clay	35
Whiting	10
Red iron oxide	2·5

(*Courtesy of Paul Barron, West Surrey College of Art and Design, Farnham, Surrey.*)

This felspathic temmoku gives a fine rich black glaze when used moderately thickly and not reduced too heavily. Where the glaze runs thinner in the firing (for instance on rims, throwing ridges and ribs of handles) it changes to a rusty-brown crystalline colour. In very heavy reduction and when used more thinly, the glaze takes on an overall iron-brown colour. In oxidation it tends to produce a very satisfactory plain black glaze. Its fairly high clay content allows it to be used as a raw glaze on leather-hard pottery, but this also means that it must not be applied too thickly to biscuit, otherwise there is some risk of it crawling. Generally, the higher the glaze is fired within its suggested range, the better its quality.

Although the London clay in this recipe is a rather local material, this recipe should work well with many red earthenware clays, but the best results will come from the most fusible clays. (A good test for fusibility is to fire the earthenware clay in a stoneware firing. The more bloated and melted the clay becomes the more suitable it will be for use in recipes of this type.)

Analyses of Materials Used in Glazes and Bodies in this Chapter

Clays	SiO_2	Al_2O_3	Fe_2O_3	TiO_2	CaO	MgO	K_2O	Na_2O	($K_2O + Na_2O$)	Loss
EOBB/Y (W.B.B.)	51·4	32·0	1·2	0·9	0·2	0·3	1·6	0·1	(1·7)	12·3
Kalbrite 2K (W.B.B.)	56·17	38·4	1·82	1·3	0·24	0·46	1·42	0·18	(1·6)	
BKS (H) (W.B.B.)	77·3	14·2	0·5	1·5	0·2	0·2	1·3	0·4	(1·7)	4·3
Hymod SM (E.C.C.)	74·0	15·0	0·8	1·5	0·1	0·3	1·6	0·3	(1·9)	6·4
BBV (W.B.B.)	71·3	18·8	0·8	1·5	0·2	0·3	1·9	0·3	(2·2)	4·9
Grolleg china clay (E.C.C.)	47·7	37·2	0·7	0·03	0·1	0·25	1·95	0·1	(2·05)	12·06
Molochite (Wengers)	54·5	42·5	0·75	0·08	0·1	0·1	1·75	0·1	(1·85)	
Felspars etc.										
Potash felspar	64·5	19·1	0·07		0·2	0·1	12·8	2·4	(15·2)	0·5
Cornish stone (synthetic)	72·9	14·93	0·13	0·02	2·06	0·09	3·81	4·0	(7·81)	2·06
Nepheline syenite (North Cape)	55·9	24·1	0·09		1·3		8·9	7·7	(16·6)	
Others										
Talc	34·8	1·3	5·6		0·4	34·5				21·1
Dolomite	0·73		1·25		31·25	19·88				46·9

	SiO$_2$	Al$_2$O$_3$	Fe$_2$O$_3$	TiO$_2$	CaO	MgO	K$_2$O	Na$_2$O	(K$_2$O + Na$_2$O)	Loss
Wollastonite	50·9	0·25	0·55	0·05	46·9	0·1				
Whiting					55·78	0·14				
Flint	98·	0·82								

Notes: SM is no longer available in powdered form, but can still be bought in the shredded state, although only in very large quantities. The 'synthetic' Cornish stone is actually a mixture of Scandinavian felspars and quartz, but true Cornish stone (Hard Purple grade) can still be obtained from Harrison Mayer Ltd., (see suppliers' list on page 87 for address). Genuine Cornish stone gives better results in glazes than the synthetic variety. These analyses are for the materials that I use in my own pottery. Different suppliers use different sources for the raw materials they sell but they usually publish analyses for their own particular felspars, talcs etc, in their catalogues, and these are the analyses that should be used in calculations.

Southern celadon clays

It is possible to copy Southern celadon clays by adding fine iron oxide or ochre to a white felspathic porcelain body — this approach was used by Bernard Leach for the 'porcellanous stoneware' he once made at his St Ives pottery.[34] This is a rather expensive way of making a 'grey porcelain' but it is probably the only way of making a porcelain that is at the same time high in iron (about 2% is ideal) and low in titanium — a most important feature of genuine Chekiang celadon bodies. However, if one can accept the more pronounced greyness that TiO$_2$ gives to a porcelain body, cheaper, simpler and much more plastic bodies can be made by adding nepheline syenite to high-silica ball clays, using a general recipe of 90—80 parts ball clay to 10—20 parts nepheline syenite. This range can give bodies identical in analysis to Southern celadon clays (except for the extra titanium dioxide).

Siliceous ball clay 'porcelains'

Clays of this type show very good technical qualities, with reasonable plasticity, low shrinkage, good glaze-fit, as well as a tendency to re-oxidize to the same warm iron-tones seen with genuine Chinese porcelain and celadon clays. Ball clay porcelains can be very vitreous and tough after firings as low as 1220°C, and can usually be fired safely to 1280°C, which was probably the upper limit for Southern celadons. Although these ball clay porcelains can contain at least as much flux, and are fired nearly as high as white Chinese porcelains, they show no signs of translucency. This, however, is also a feature of most Southern celadon bodies. Like the Chinese bodies, these clays can often be raw-glazed when quite dry, as long as an interval is left between glazing the insides and outsides. Some shapes, however, such as wide bowls and dishes, should not be raw-glazed, as they tend to crack with this treatment.

When creating recipes for this type of body, those ball clays that contain the most silica and least potash + soda should be mixed with the highest quantities of nepheline syenite (up to 20% of the total mix); while siliceous clays with rather less silica and more flux can use quantities nearer 10%. The lower limit of silica in a siliceous ball clay can be taken as about 65% SiO_2 in the unfired clay analysis. Siliceous ball clays are unhealthy materials and good precautions should be taken to avoid inhaling the dust, which contains quantities of very fine silica.

'Northern' stoneware bodies

It might be thought that clays of this type should be easier to imitate than celadon-bodies because they seem to be nearer to the 'ordinary' stonewares that most potters use. However, it is surprisingly hard to find stoneware clays that are both as fine in texture and as low in fluxes as typical Chinese clays — especially as almost all fire clays have to be disqualified because of their high pyrites content. Pure ball clay bodies are not the complete answer either, because their shrinkage in drying and firing is unacceptably high. Some success can be had with bodies made by adding ball-milled fire clays in the slip form to dry ball clays in the right proportions to make a plastic clay (the ball-milling disperses the iron evenly throughout the body). This can give bodies with all the colour and character of Northern stonewares, but the range between the two major body faults of crazing and shattering seem rather narrow — possibly because the clays are so low in fluxes. Simply from the evidence of their analyses some American clays seem much nearer to this type of body than English clays and it may be easier to make this type of stoneware in the USA than it is here.

White Chinese porcelains

An account of the factors involved in the imitation of Chinese porcelains with Western materials would constitute a whole book to do justice to the subject, for much of the history of Western ceramics from the early eighteenth century onwards has been concerned with this problem. Even so, it was not until the late nineteenth century that hard porcelains began to be calculated directly from the ideal oxide proportions of Chinese and Japanese porcelains. True *micaceous* hard-paste porcelains seem only to have been made experimentally in the West at Sèvres in the 1880s and Stoke-on-Trent in the early years of this century. Both research projects produced fascinating papers [10, 32] and the work of George Vogt at Sèvres, particularly, resulted in the most complete and detailed account of the technology of Chinese porcelain production ever written. The Sèvres and the Staffordshire porcelains were designed to mature at the typical firing temperatures for nineteenth century Chinese porcelain of about 1280°C, but neither body became established commercially.

Modern hard-paste porcelains are made from mixtures of potash felspar, quartz and china clay, and the only mica they contain is about 5—8% from the china clay. Most modern porcelains have been deliberately designed to be as near as possible to Far Eastern porcelains in their analyses, and bodies of this type can be calculated from the analyses of Chinese porcelains in this book, using the methods described for glazes. The 'simultaneous' method of calculation that takes the flux in the china clays into account gives the most accurate results, but, because these recipes do not have the advantage of a high content of fine mica, they tend to be rather non-plastic. Also Chinese porcelains are rather siliceous and tend to give recipes low in clay.

Using mica in porcelains and glazes

The subject of mica in porcelains and glazes is only just beginning to be explored again by Western potters, but there are certain problems involved with its use that should be mentioned. Firstly, the crystal structure of mica makes it very resistant to grinding and it is therefore difficult to obtain mica fine enough to use in porcelain bodies. Also, mica is a recognized health hazard, and, like most silicate dusts, it is the finest grades that are the most risky. To these problems can be added the fact that mica is three to four times the price of felspar and it is difficult to buy mica in quantities of less than one ton. In short the difficulties in using pure mica in ceramics are considerable and it is probably better to look for clays and rocks that are similar to those used in the Far East and that already contain white mica in a form fine enough to be useful in porcelains or glazes. Finally, however, there is always the consideration that it may not be very long before it becomes possible to import pottery raw materials directly from China, and the availability of petuntse particularly, would allow Western potters to work with one of the world's most versatile ceramic raw materials.

Fig. 30 'Chicken-head' stoneware ewer, (height 9·5 inches). About 4th century A.D.

Grey-green, near-celadon glaze with added dots of iron oxide, Yüeh ware. These stylish and finely-made ewers show the high standards achieved by the Yüeh potters of South China as early as the Six Dynasties era (A.D. 265—581). The thin glaze probably has a composition somewhere between the lime and lime-alkali types. Both glaze and clay must be siliceous enough to avoid crazing. The ewer has been reduction fired (probably between 1200 and 1230°C) and in places the body has re-oxidized beneath the glaze. Again the glaze recipe may have been some combination of the body clay with limestone or lime, though less lime and more clay than in the 'proto-Yüeh' example in Fig. 2. *British Museum*

8 Glaze Analyses

Green high-lime glazes

('Proto-porcelain' and Japanese Karatsu glazes)

Date	SiO_2	Al_2O_3	Fe_2O_3	TiO_2	CaO	MgO	K_2O	Na_2O	$(K_2O + Na_2O)$	CuO
Han[3]	54·17	14·16	4·36		19·05	2·02		5·49(?)	(5·49)	
6 Dynasties[19]	55·5	16·1	5·6	0·3	18·8	1·0		2·7	(2·7)	
6 Dynasties[19]	52·0	17·5	5·1		20·5	2·0		2·9	(2·9)	
6 Dynasties[19]	58·4	17·0	4·4	1·1	14·8	0·1		3·0	(3·0)	1·2
6 Dynasties[19]	56·0	15·4	1·6	0·7	22·2	0·1		3·7	(3·7)	0·3

These glazes were used in Southern China from about the first to the sixth centuries A.D. (see Figs. 2 and 30) and are of the type believed to have been made from a mixture of about two parts body clay to one of lime (and possibly containing some ash). They are typically low-silica, high-alumina glazes containing about 20% of lime (CaO) and maturing at about 1200°C. They are prone to run with overfiring and show the 'patterning' and dullness typical of high-lime, high-alumina stoneware glazes. They are the ancestors of the Southern celadons. The next two glazes are the chemically similar Japanese Karatsu glazes. These are more likely to be made from clay and ash recipes and may be similar to early North Chinese high-lime glazes.

SiO_2	Al_2O_3	Fe_2O_3	TiO_2	CaO	MgO	$(K_2O + Na_2O)$	MnO
60·57	14·0	2·19	0·26	16·0	3·38	3·49	0·5
61·36	10·36	1·56	0·25	18·36	3·7	4·43	0·5

Transitional Chinese celadons and Kuan glaze

Date	SiO_2	Al_2O_3	Fe_2O_3	TiO_2	CaO	MgO	K_2O	Na_2O	$(K_2O + Na_2O)$	MnO	P_2O_5
5 Dynasties[8]	59·4	15·96	1·8	0·39	16·04	2·04	3·43	0·32	(3·75)	0·62	
Northern Sung[8]	63·25	16·82	1·42	0·23	13·00	1·09	3·26	0·57	(3·83)	0·43	
Kuan glaze Southern Sung[5]	62·98	15·31	1·08	0·03	14·54	1·02	4·00	0·16	(4·16)		0·52

The first two glazes represent some stage between the 'proto-porcelain' glazes and the best Southern celadons (Fig. 5). They show the increasing percentages of silica and decreasing percentages of lime which were the main improvements necessary in the evolution of Southern celadons. The Kuan glaze is of this same general type but the lower figures for such 'impurities' as TiO_2, Fe_2O_3 and MnO, show that much finer raw material have been used in the recipe, which could have been some combination of Chekiang white earth, lime and a considerable amount of wood ash, (say 20%). These glazes probably mature between 1200 and 1240°C.

'Classic' Chekiang celadons of the Sung Dynasties[7, 8]

	SiO_2	Al_2O_3	Fe_2O_3	TiO_2	CaO	MgO	K_2O	Na_2O	$(K_2O + Na_2O)$	MnO	P_2O_5
Sung	68·02	14·14	0·91		9·88	0·77	4·41	1·54	(5·95)		
Sung	68·00	14·51	1·32		9·05		5·36	1·41	(6·77)		
Sung	68·29	14·96	1·08		11·38		3·53	0·48	(4·02)		
Sung	65·73	14·58	2·3	0·1	9·74	0·92	4·94	1·27	(6·21)	0·2	
Sung	66·33	14·28	0·99	0·03	11·34	1·17	4·35	0·99	(5·34)	0·36	
Sung	68·63	14·32	1·01	0·12	10·02	0·32	4·31	1·08	(5·39)	0·12	
Sung	67·0	14·71	1·01	0·14	11·51	0·65	4·26	0·54	(4·8)	0·2	
Sung	68·6	14·28	0·73	0·02	10·4	0·4	4·97	0·14	(5·11)		0·14
Sung	67·5	14·92	1·08	0·48	9·5	0·45	5·72		(5·72)		0·23

These nine Chekiang celadons of the finest quality were fired in a strongly reducing atmosphere at temperatures between about 1220°C and 1260°C and they represent the greatest achievement in glaze design in South China in the Sung Dynasty (see Fig. 6). Where there are no figures given for the trace oxides such as TiO_2, MnO and P_2O_5, this does not necessarily mean they are absent from the glazes. Some glazes have been analysed more thoroughly than others, and those glazes that show figures for these oxides will give some idea of the possible amounts of these oxides in other glazes. The next group of Southern celadons are those whose analyses fall somewhat short of this ideal balance, particularly in the silica-alumina figures, and this suggests that more aluminous 'white earths' may have been used in the recipes.

More aluminous Chekiang celadons[7, 8]

	SiO_2	Al_2O_3	Fe_2O_3	TiO_2	CaO	MgO	K_2O	Na_2O	$(K_2O + Na_2O)$	MnO
Sung	68·77	15·66	1·05		9·05		4·83	0·82	(5·6)	
Sung	65·27	16·89	0·92		11·93	0·76	3·68	0·52	(4·2)	
Sung	69·16	15·4	0·95		8·39	0·61	4·87	0·32	(5·09)	
Sung	65·63	15·92	1·1		9·94	0·86	5·06	1·12	(6·18)	0·32
Sung	65·31	16·61	0·83		12·24	0·82	3·75	0·45	(4·2)	0·08

The glazes in this class that contain 68% and 69% SiO_2 (as well the high alumina figures) probably mature above 1250°C. The remaining oxides show the same balance of fluxes as the classic glazes. The celadon glazes of the next dynasties (Yüan and Ming), however, show an increasing divergence from the ideal balance.

Post-Sung Southern celadons

	SiO_2	Al_2O_3	Fe_2O_3	TiO_2	CaO	MgO	K_2O	Na_2O	$(K_2O + Na_2O)$	MnO
Yüan[8]	67·41	16·74	1·51	0·18	6·83	0·63	5·49	1·16	(6·65)	0·45
Yüan[36]	65·7	13·7	1·46	trace	11·45	1·6	4·2	1·82	(6·02)	trace
Ming[22]	65·0	14·33	1·39	1·39	10·09	1·55	5·61	0·81	(6·42)	trace
Ming[8]	67·57	15·00	1·44	trace	6·28	1·72	6·48	1·14	(7·62)	0·14

These four glazes show that Southern celadons became higher in alkalis, iron and magnesia after the end of the Sung dynasties. This may have been caused by the use of increasing amounts of wood ash in the recipes, but the celadon clays used at this time also seem unusually high in alkalis. The two glazes below are modern celadons that have survived to be used in the 20th-century Chekiang kilns and are made from mixtures of 'purple earth', 'white earth', slaked lime and rice-husk ash.

Modern Chekiang celadons[7, 8]

	SiO_2	Al_2O_3	Fe_2O_3	TiO_2	CaO	MgO	K_2O	Na_2O	$(K_2O + Na_2O)$	MnO
Celadon 1959	65·82	15·53	1·4		12·54		4·33	0·46	(4·79)	
Celadon 1961	67·31	12·03	1·06	0·17	14·95	0·26	3·55	0·62	(4·17)	0·04

These modern glazes have lime percentages approaching those of the pre-Sung celadons, with all that this implies in terms of limited maturing range and dullness or glassiness of appearance. With the aid of analysis it has been a relatively simple matter for the modern Chinese potters to correct this drift back toward the 'transitional' type of glaze, and re-establish the 'ideal' celadon oxide balance.

The last class of celadons are the modern felspathic type that give a similar, though somewhat 'heavier' quality, to the lime-alkali types. These glazes are higher-firing (1280°–1305°C), more siliceous and low in clay and alumina. They cannot usually be applied to the raw clay like true celadons.

Modern felspathic Chinese and Japanese celadons

	SiO$_2$	Al$_2$O$_3$	TiO$_2$	Fe$_2$O$_3$	CaO	MgO	K$_2$O	Na$_2$O	(K$_2$O + Na$_2$O)
1956 Kiangsi Celadon[6]	71·0	13·5	0·18	1·95	5·0	0·46	4·4	3·8	(8·2)
Japanese[23]	73·7	12·5		1·66	4·45		7·8		(7·8)
Celadons[24] 1920s	73·3	12·3		1·67	5·9		7·2		(7·2)

For some reason it is necessary to use more iron in felspathic celadons to achieve the same intensity of colour as the lower-firing 'true' celadons. The silica content of the Japanese glazes is deliberately excessive for the firing temperature, with the undissolved silica producing the semi-opacity necessary for a good celadon. The absence of titanium oxide ensures a good blue colour for the glazes, which were designed to imitate the finest Chekiang Sung celadons that were probably made at Ta yao and are called 'Kinuta' celadons by the Japanese.

These 32 celadons and near-celadons represent the most important series of analyses made of any one type of Far Eastern glaze and it seems very likely that the transparent porcelain and stoneware glazes of both North and South China represent a similar lime to lime-alkali evolution. The following analyses of Chinese Chüns show that these too are mainly of the lime-alkali type.

Northern Chinese Chün glazes of the Sung Dynasty

	SiO$_2$	Al$_2$O$_3$	TiO$_2$	Fe$_2$O$_3$	CaO	MgO	K$_2$O	Na$_2$O	(K$_2$O + Na$_2$O)	P$_2$O$_5$
Sung[28] Chün	67·0	13·2	0·5	1·62	9·34	1·1	4·48	0·46	(4·94)	0·4
Sung Chün	67·0	14·12	0·21	1·68	9·95	0·67	5·0		(5·0)	1·31

These two northern Chün glazes are almost indistinguishable from the 'ideal' Southern celadons. The high P$_2$O$_5$% must account for the 'Chün effect'. The next two Chüns are described as 'light green' and 'bluish violet' Chüns and have similar SiO$_2$ + Al$_2$O$_3$ totals although one is high-silica and the other high-alumina glaze:

	SiO$_2$	Al$_2$O$_3$	TiO$_2$	Fe$_2$O$_3$	CaO	MgO	K$_2$O	Na$_2$O	(K$_2$O + Na$_2$O)	P$_2$O$_5$
Light Green[5]	67·4	15·8	0·3	0·6	11·8		2·6	1·0	(3·6)	0·5
Bluish Violet[5]	72·8	9·94	0·07	1·58	8·8	1·5	4·57		(4·57)	0·5

These four are phosphatic Chüns, but there is a type of Chün glaze where lead is used to produce opalescence. The use of lead in glazes is a very ancient Northern practice and Dr Sundius studied a number of high-fired Northern glazes that spectroscopic analysis showed to contain small, but significant amounts of lead. These two lead-containing Chüns were not among the glazes analysed for *Sung Sherds*, but they are true high-firing Chüns that have some similarities to copper reds made hundreds of years later in South China — that is, they contain a fair amount of lead and are rather low in alumina.

	SiO_2	Al_2O_3	Fe_2O_3	TiO_2	CaO	MgO	K_2O	Na_2O	$(K_2O + Na_2O)$	PbO	CuO
Chun	70·05	8·21	1·78	0·6	8·14	1·43	7·07		(7·07)	2·73	0·1
Chun	66·05	8·53	1·69	0·02	7·23	1·08	5·44		(5·44)	9·09	0·06

These glazes may have originally been closer in analysis than they seem now. It is possible that more lead has volatilized from the first glaze than the second, making it ultimately higher in silica. More than ten per cent lead oxide may have been used in the original recipes.

Porcelain glazes

Unfortunately no analyses of Eastern porcelain glazes exist that were used earlier than the 19th century. However, it is very likely that the earliest porcelain glazes showed the same development as the celadons, with the difference that the iron and titanium contents were generally lower. That modern Chinese and Japanese porcelain glazes are of the true celadon type is shown by these four analyses of 19th century porcelain glazes:

	SiO_2	Al_2O_3	Fe_2O_3	TiO_2	CaO	MgO	K_2O	Na_2O	$(K_2O + Na_2O)$	MnO	P_2O_5
Late 19th Chinese[10]	69·43	14·35	0·78	trace	9·62	0·44	3·3	2·12	(5·42)		
Early 19th Chinese[35]	68·0	12·0	traces		14·0		6·0		(6·0)		
Late 19th Japanese[22]	68·5	14·3	0·43		10·6		4·62	1·24	(5·86)		0·33
Late 19th Japanese[22]	70·7	13·9	0·87		9·55		2·13	2·5	(4·63)		0·18

All four glazes were probably made by mixing about 80 parts of porcelain stone with limestone or lime and a small amount of ash. The glazes with the highest SiO_2/Al_2O_3 totals would mature at about 1280° to 1300°C.

Iron glazes

The composition of Chinese temmokus is unknown at the moment and the glaze analyses in this section are of modern Chinese, Japanese and Western glazes that seem to share common characteristics with real Chinese temmokus. This is most true of the Albany slip clays found in New York state.

Analyses of Albany slip glazes (fired)[30, 31]

SiO_2	Al_2O_3	TiO_2	Fe_2O_3	CaO	MgO	K_2O	Na_2O	$(K_2O + Na_2O)$
63·5	16·3	0·4	5·7	6·4	2·9	3·6	0·9	(4·5)
64·0	16·7	?	3·5	6·3	3·7	5·0		(5·0)
62·5	16·7	?	6·6	6·4	2·8	3·64	1·21	(4·85)
61·0	17·0	1·1	6·3	6·35	3·55	3·25		(3·25)
64·8	16·3	?	5·85	6·4	3·04	3·5		(3·5)

These glazes are noticeably higher in alumina and lower in silica than most celadons and porcelain glazes. Glazes made up to these analyses give results very similar to Northern temmokus in oxidizing to neutral firings above 1260°C, and applied thickly in strong reduction, they can look like some Chien temmokus. Albany slips can actually display quite remarkable differences in appearance according to whether they are thick or thin, high or low fired, oxidized or reduced, or on light or dark bodies. The differences encompass a great many typical Chinese temmokus, including the very attractive, dull, rusty-bronze glaze used in both North and South China from the Sung dynasty until at least the end of the nineteenth century. Its most familiar modern use is for French porcelain coffee and tea sets. The one analysis of a genuine Chinese glaze of this type dates from the late nineteenth century when it was used on the outside of porcelain cups and bowls and known to the Chinese as the 'dead leaf' glaze.[10] This glaze was re-created successfully by George Vogt at Sèvres and this may explain how it came to be used on French domestic porcelain. It is similar to Albany slip in analysis, though slightly more siliceous and lower in MgO:

SiO_2	Al_2O_3	TiO_2	Fe_2O_3	CaO	MgO	K_2O	Na_2O	$(K_2O + Na_2O)$
66·67	16·67	0·36	3·75	7·35	0·5	3·14	1·53	(4·67)

Similar in analysis to both Albany slip and the 'dead leaf' glaze is Kimaichi stone,[16] a widely used Japanese glaze material that gives a streaky brown/black glaze when used alone, and a true temmoku with a few per cent of common ash:

SiO_2	Al_2O_3	Fe_2O_3	TiO_2	CaO	MgO	K_2O	Na_2O	$(K_2O + Na_2O)$	MnO
63·72	16·5	6·11	0·65	5·6	1·95	1·41	3·82	(5·23)	0·24

The presence of magnesia in most of these glazes means that they need to be fired above 1260°C for their best character to appear. Magnesia does not seem to start acting as a flux until this temperature is reached, but once it does, its action is extremely powerful and it gives the glazes the kind of richness usually associated with lead. Underfired temmokus containing magnesia are particularly dull, and the difference made by a few degrees of temperature is striking.

Mashiko stone Kaki is slightly different, having a high silica content and, therefore, more likely to produce rusty crystalline colours with iron. This material was made famous by Shoji Hamada and is now widely used by other potters in Japan.

Mashiko stone Kaki glaze (and with 10% common ash)[16]

SiO_2	Al_2O_3	Fe_2O_3	TiO_2	CaO	MgO	K_2O	Na_2O	$(K_2O + Na_2O)$	MnO	P_2O_5
68·0	14·3	6·55	0·71	3·7	1·92	1·8	2·46	(4·26)	0·2	0·23
66·0	13·9	6·3	0·61	5·75	2·05		4·5	(4·5)	0·31	0·4

The second analysis is based on a recipe of 90% Mashiko stone, 10% wood ash. This should give a good, rich, black temmoku at about 1280°C. The Mashiko stone used by itself is most suitable as an over-glaze and gives excellent results on the glassier celadons, porcelain glazes, and particularly, on black temmokus.

The last three iron glazes are the low-firing, 'mirror black' glazes, popular in China from the eighteenth century onwards, but of a type sometimes seen on the very rare 'black Ting' wares of Sung China. The first glaze was in use at Ching-tê Chên in the 1880s, the second is an adaptation of the same glaze made at Sèvres, and the third is a modern mirror-black glaze used at Ching-tê Chên in the 1950s:

	SiO_2	Al_2O_3	Fe_2O_3	TiO_2	CaO	MgO	$(K_2O + Na_2O)$	MnO	CoO
19th Century[10] mirror-black	61·9	11·36	9·15	trace	10·65	0·1	(3·3)	3·0	0·43
Sèvres black[10]	63·0	11·8	9·7	not tested	9·1	0·1	(3·45)	2·45	0·45
Utzen black[6]	61·5	13·0	6·5	0·23	13·0	1·5	(4·07)	0·31	

The first glaze matures at about 1200°C, as its low silica and alumina total suggests. Mirror-black glazes can be used in oxidation or reduction. Because of their fluid character they will not take on-glaze decoration and if they are applied too thickly they tend to crystallize slightly on the surface, and will also be prone to running. With a medium thickness of glaze on a smooth body they show a remarkably even mirror-black glaze. The

Sèvres glaze is an adaptation made by Vogt of the Chinese glaze designed to make it slightly higher firing.

Felspathic temmokus

Like virtually all the Chinese glazes in this chapter these mirror-black glazes are of the lime or lime-alkali type. Most Western temmokus used by studio potters are felspathic and of a totally different character, particularly in their tendency to show strong rust-red colours where thin. This 'black breaking to red' is often thought to be the hallmark of 'real' temmokus, although it is a phenomenon rarely seen in Northern temmokus, and, in the case of Chien bowls of Fukien province, the thin glaze is brown rather than rust-coloured.

Analyses of Chinese clays

These clay analyses trace the development of porcelain in China from the Han dynasty to the present day, beginning with Chekiang 'proto-porcelain' and concluding with a typical white porcelain made at Ching-tê Chên in the 1950s. The first six analyses show the development of Chekiang celadon bodies and the last five are of translucent white porcelains, mostly from Kiangsi province.

	SiO_2	Al_2O_3	Fe_2O_3	TiO_2	CaO	MgO	K_2O	Na_2O	$(K_2O + Na_2O)$	MnO
Han Proto-porcelain[19]	73·68	17·19	4·47	0·76	0·2	0·46	2·8	0·22	(3·02)	0·02
Transitional celadon body[8]	74·23	18·62	2·27	0·42	0·54	0·59	2·77	0·48	(3·25)	0·02
Sung celadon body[7]	73·22	19·10	2·19	0·32	0·3		3·62	1·09	(4·71)	
Sung celadon body[8]	69·76	22·39	2·36		0·4		4·42	0·75	(5·17)	
Yüan celadon body[8]	70·77	20·13	1·63	0·16	0·17	0·74	5·5	0·82	(6·32)	0·07
Ming celadon body[8]	70·18	20·47	1·71	0·19	0·16	0·29	6·02	0·97	(6·99)	0·1

These body analyses show the same gradual decrease in iron and titanium oxides and increase in potash and soda that can be seen in the analyses of the glazes used with them (see glaze analyses page 78). The earliest bodies may have been naturally high in iron, while the later bodies may be mixtures of white and purple earths.

White Porcelain Bodies (mainly from Ching-tê Chên)

	SiO_2	Al_2O_3	Fe_2O_3	TiO_2	CaO	MgO	K_2O	Na_2O	$(K_2O + Na_2O)$
White Sung[5]	70·58	21·43	0·91	0·02	1·14	0·91	4·7	0·23	(4·93)
K'ang Hsi (17th—18th C.)[37]	71·82	23·04			0·63	trace	1·89	2·12	(4·01)
Early 19th C.[35]	69·6	22·06	1·31		0·76		3·55	2·68	(6·23)
Late 19th C. (Imperial factory)[10]	69·46	23·68	0·8		0·18		2·8	3·04	(5·84)
1950s body (calculated)	72·0	23·4	0·75	0·06	0·16	0·17	1·55	1·82	(3·37)

The last two porcelains are definitely micaceous, the early 19th century body may be micaceous too, for it uses petuntses and kaolins with the same names as those that have since been shown to contain considerable mica. The mineralogy of Chinese porcelains made earlier than the 19th century is still unknown.

Chinese stoneware bodies

These North Chinese stoneware bodies were used in the Sung dynasty and show the low-alkali and high-alumina figures typical of ordinary Chinese stonewares. The relatively high CaO figures are unusual in high-firing clays, but whether they are natural to this type of clay or represent some attempt to lower the maturing temperature of the bodies (or even to reduce crazing) is another 'unknown'.

	SiO_2	Al_2O_3	Fe_2O_3	TiO_2	MgO	CaO	K_2O	Na_2O	$(K_2O + Na_2O)$
Northern temmoku body[5]	60.9	32.0	1.9	1.6	0.1	1.7	1.5	0.3	(1.8)
Northern Chün body[5]	64.9	28.3	2.0	0.9	0.1	1.0	1.9	0.3	(2.2)
Northern celadon body[5]	63.7	29.01	1.78	0.94	0.62	1.12	1.84	0.45	(2.29)

These Northern stonewares are generally of very fine and even particle size and are, therefore, rather different from most stoneware clays used by craft potters in the West. These Chinese clays have something of the character of Western fire clays but they lack the iron pyrites that produce 'spotting' in the Western clays when fired in reducing conditions.

Calculating bodies from analyses of Chinese clays

These Chinese clay analyses can be used as bases for calculation in the same way as glazes, but it must be stressed that good results are far less certain. An oxide analysis is only one aspect of a clay's nature and such information as particle size distribution, and general mineralogy is at least as important as an oxide analysis for understanding a clay properly. Even so, it is surprising how successful clay bodies calculated from Chinese clays and porcelains can be, and the successes can make up for the occasional disasters!

Appendix 1–Suppliers' List

UK suppliers

Clays
English China Clays Sales Co. Ltd., St. Austell, Cornwall, do not supply customers directly with quantities of clay less than ten tonnes, but the following E.C.C. agents will deal in lesser amounts:
Anchor Chemical Co. Ltd., Clayton, Manchester, M11 4SR.
Fordamin (Sales) Co. Ltd., Free Wharf, Brighton Road, Shoreham-by-Sea, Sussex.
Somerville Agencies Ltd., Meadowside Street, Renfrew.
Whitfield and Sons Ltd., 23 Albert Street, Newcastle-under-Lyme, Staffs. ST5 1JP.

Watts, Blake, Bearne & Co. Ltd. is the other major ball clay and china clay mining company in the UK and they will supply quantities of clay above one tonne. Their address is:
Watts Blake Bearne & Co. Ltd., Park House, Courtenay Park, Newton Abbot, Devon TQ12 4PS.

Most of the other suppliers of pottery materials sell the more popular E.C.C. and W.B.B. ball clays and china clays, although often by names or codes different from those used by the original suppliers. The analyses of the clays should show which clays have been re-named.

All other raw materials and pottery equipment
Podmore Ceramics Ltd., 105 Minet Road, London SW9 7UH. Tel. 01-737-3636
Podmore and Son Ltd., Shelton, Stoke, Staffs. Tel. 0782-24571
The Fulham Pottery Ltd., 210 New King's Road, London SW6. Tel. 01-736-1188
Potclays Ltd., Brickkiln Lane, Etruria, Stoke, Staffs. Tel. 0782-29816

Ferro (GB) Ltd., Wombourne, Wolverhampton, Staffs. Tel. 09077-4144
Harrison Mayer Ltd., Meir, Stoke, Staffs. Tel. 0782-31611
Wengers Ltd., Etruria, Stoke, Staffs. Tel. 0782-25126
Degg Industrial Minerals Ltd., Phoenix Works, Webberley Lane, Longton,
    Stoke-on-Trent ST3 1RJ. Tel. 0782-316077

US suppliers

American Art Clay Co. Inc., 4717 W. 16th St., Indianapolis, Ind. 46222
Arch T. Flower Co. Queen St. & Ivy Hill Rd., Philadelphia, PA 19118
Bog Town Clay, 75—J Mendel Ave., S.W. Atlanta, GA 30336
Castle Clay Products, 1055 S. Fox St., Denver, CO 80223
Cedar Heights Clay Co., 50 Portsmouth Road, Oak Hill, Ohio 45656
Clay Art Center, 40 Beech St., Port Chester, NY 10573
Cole Ceramics Labs, North Eastern Office, Box 248, Sharon, CONN.
    06069
Creek Turn Pottery Supply, Route 38, Hainesport, NJ 08036
Eagle Ceramics, 12266 Wilkins Ave., Rockville, MD 20852 and 1300 W. 9th
    St., Cleveland, OH 44113
Edgar Plastic Kaolin Co., Edgar, Putnam Co., FLA 32049
George Fetzer Ceramic Supplies, 1205 17th Ave., Columbus, OH 43211
Firehouse Ceramics, 238 Mulberry St., New York, NY 10012
Georgia Kaolin Co., 433 N. Broad St., Elizabeth, NJ 07207
Hammill & Gillespie, Box 104, Livingston, NJ 07039
Leslie Ceramics Supply Co., 1212 San Pablo Ave., Berkeley, CA 94706
Metropolitan Refractories, Tidewater Terminal, So. Kearny, NJ 07032
Minnesota Clay Co., 8001 Grand Ave. S., Bloomington, MINN. 55420
Newton Potters Supply, Inc., 96 Rumford Ave., Newton, MA 02165
Rovin Ceramics, 6912 Schaefer Rd., Dearborn, MICH 48216
The Salem Craftsmen's Guild, 3 Alvin Pl., Upper Montclair, NJ 07043 and
    1042 Salem Rd., Union, NJ 07083
Sculpture House, 38 E. 30th St., New York, NY 10016
Standard Ceramic Supply Co., Box 4435, Pittsburgh, PA 15205
Trinity Ceramic Supply Co., 9016 Diplomacy Row, Dallas, Texas, 75235
Western Ceramic Supply, 1601 Howard St., San Francisco, CA 94103
Westwood Ceramic Supply Co., 14400 Lomitas Ave., City of Industry,
    CA 91744
Jack D. Wolfe Co., 724 Meeker Ave., Brooklyn, NY 11222

Appendix 2–Analyses of Glaze Materials

Typical Analyses of Eastern and Western Porcelain Stones and Felspars

	SiO_2	Al_2O_3	Fe_2O_3	TiO_2	CaO	MgO	K_2O	Na_2O	$(K_2O + Na_2O)$	P_2O_5	Loss
China											
Nan-kang stone (kaolinized petuntse)	75·06	16·01	0·41	0·05	0·28	0·6	3·30	1·97	(5·27)	—	2·21
Chekiang white earth (fired)	77·21	16·46	0·51	—	0·55	0·3	4·76	0·2	(4·96)	—	—
Kiangsi glaze stone	75·77	14·62	0·32	0·06	1·28	0·84	2·24	2·6	(4·84)	—	2·51
Japan											
Amakusa stone	77·21	15·13	0·36	—	0·17	0·18	3·12	trace	(3·12)	—	3·9
Fukishima felspar	65·26	19·1	0·09	—	0·26	0·23	9·82	4·6	(14·42)	—	0·36
UK (Imported, except for Harrison Mayer's Cornish stones)											
Cornish stone (hard and mild purple)	72·5	15·4	0·13	0·05	1·4	0·08	4·95	3·7	(8·65)	0·42	1·44
Cornish stone (hard white)	73·3	16·0	0·2	0·05	0·87	0·17	5·1	1·57	(6·67)	0·35	2·26
potash felspar (Harrison Mayer)	65·19	18·98	0·12	—	0·47	—	11·81	2·88	(14·7)	—	0·36
Cornish stone* (Podmore & Sons)	72·9	14·93	0·13	0·02	2·06	0·09	3·81	4·00	(7·81)	—	0·61
potash felspar (Podmore & Sons)	68·2	17·5	0·2	—	0·25	0·12	10·3	2·5	(12·8)	—	—
mineralized stone* (Wengers Ltd)	75·4	14·5	0·18	—	0·25	—	4·3	4·8	(9·1)	—	—
potash felspar (Wengers Ltd)	66·11	18·26	0·1	—	0·76	0·1	10·38	3·75	(14·13)	—	—

* These materials are blends of felspar and quartz and do not seem to give to glazes quite the same characteristics typical of genuine Cornish stone (depth, slight opalescence). This may be because they lack the small percentages of phosphorous and fluorine found in true Cornish stones.

	SiO_2	Al_2O_3	Fe_2O_3	TiO_2	CaO	MgO	K_2O	Na_2O	$(K_2O + Na_2O)$	P_2O_5	Loss
US											
Plastic Vitrox	75·56	14·87	0·09	—	0·22	0·2	6·81	0·29	(7·1)	—	2·04
Carolina stone	72·3	16·23	0·07	—	0·62	0·01	4·42	4·4	(8·82)	—	1·06
Buckingham felspar	65·58	19·6	0·01	—	0·16	0·2	12·44	2·56	(15·00)	—	0·32
Oxford felspar	69·4	17·04	0·09	—	0·38	—	7·92	3·22	(11·14)	—	0·3

This table shows that the rocks that form the basis of Chinese bodies and glazes are far lower in alkalis than Western materials, and those Chinese rocks that have been analysed mineralogically show the K_2O to be present as mica (sericite), rather than potash felspar. The Amakusa stone of Japan is probably micaceous too. True felspathic rocks are also found in Japan and many old Japanese glazes are of true felspathic composition. The two rocks still obtainable in the West that seem to be most like Chinese petuntse and Chekiang clay are hard white Cornish stone (UK) and Plastic Vitrox (US).

Appendix 3–Map of China and List of Dynasties

Dates of Chinese dynasties

Neolithic	8000–7000 B.C. to 1800–1600 B.C.
Shang	1800–1600 B.C. to about 1030 B.C.
Chou	about 1030 B.C. to 256 B.C.
Han	202 B.C. to A.D. 220
Three Kingdoms	A.D. 221 to A.D. 265
Six Dynasties	265 to 581
Sui	581 to 618
T'ang	618 to 906
Five Dynasties	907 to 960
Northern Sung	960 to 1126 (North and South China)
Southern Sung	1127 to 1279 (South China only)
Chin (Tartars)	1115 to 1234 (North China only)
Yüan (Monguls)	1260 to 1368
Ming	1368 to 1644
Ch'ing (Manchus)	1644 to 1912
Republic	1912 to 1949
People's Republic	1949 to present day

Key to the main productions of the shaded areas on the map.

(a) Cream-coloured porcelain (Ting ware)

(b) Painted and engraved white-slipped stoneware and temmoku ware (Tz'u-chou ware)

(c) Northern celadon

(d) Northern celadon, Chün ware, Ju ware and Northern temmoku

(e) Early South Chinese celadon ware (Proto-Yüeh and Yüeh ware), also Kuan ware

(f) Southern white porcelains (Ch'ing-pai ware and blue-and-white porcelains)

(g) Ordinary stonewares, mostly oxidized

(h) Temmoku ware, but also some lighter-coloured stoneware

(i) Southern celadon (mostly blue-green glazes on near-porcelain bodies), also some Kuan-type ware

(j) Chien ware tea bowls ('hare's fur' temmoku)

(k) Fukien porcelain (mainly plain white porcelain known as 'blanc-de-chine')

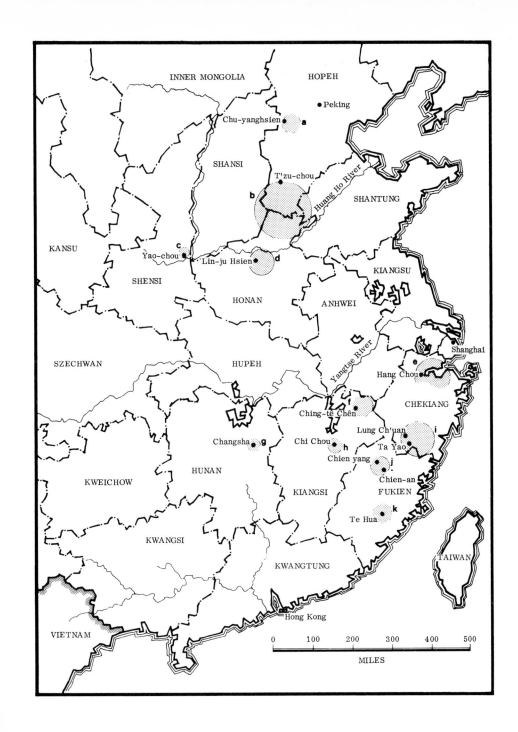

INNER MONGOLIA

HOPEH

• Peking

Chu-yanghsien • a

SHANSI

T'zu-chou •

b

Huang Ho River

SHANTUNG

KANSU

c

Yao-chou • Lin-ju Hsien • d

SHENSI

KIANGSU

HONAN

ANHWEI

SZECHWAN

HUPEH

Yangtse River

Shanghai •

Hang Chou • e

CHEKIANG

Ching-tê Chên • f

Lung Ch'uan • i

Changsha • g

Chi Chou • h

Ta Yao •

Chien yang • j

HUNAN

KIANGSI

Chien-an

FUKIEN

KWEICHOW

Te Hua • k

KWANGSI

KWANGTUNG

TAIWAN

Hong Kong

VIETNAM

0   100   200   300   400   500

MILES

Appendix 4–Bibliography

(References in the text to these books and journals are indicated by [ ]

1   Michael Cardew: *Pioneer Pottery* (Longman, Harlow, Essex, 1969; St. Martin's Press, New York, 1971)

2   F. Singer and W. L. German: *Ceramic Glazes* (Borax Consolidated, 1960)

3   H. W. Nichols: *Report on Technical Investigation of Ancient Chinese Pottery* — pages 86—94 in Berthold Laufer's book: *The Beginnings of Porcelain in China* (Chicago Natural History Museum, 1917)

4   *Meng-Chang Ling: *Chinese Ash Glaze* — American Ceramic Society Bulletin, Vol. 26 (1947) 7

5   Nils Palmegren, Nils Sundius and Walter Steger: *Sung Sherds* (Almqvist & Wiksell, Stockholm, 1963)

6   *G. L. Efremov: *Art Porcelain in the Chinese People's Republic* — Stecklo I. Keramika 13 (11) 28—30 (1956)

7   *Li Kuo-chen and Ye Hung-ming: *An Investigation of the Lung Ch'uan Celadon Glazes* — Journal of the Chinese Silicate Society, 1964, pages 1—13 (in Chinese)

8   *Chou Jen, Chang Fu-k'ang and Chêng Yung-fu: *Technical Studies of the Lung Ch'üan Celadons of Successive Dynasties* — Kao-ku hsüeh-pao, 1973, No. 1, pages 131—156 (in Chinese)

9   *Willard J. Sutton: *The Manufacture of Porcelain near Tehwa, South China* — Bulletin of the American Ceramic Society, 17, 450 (1938)

10 *George Vogt: *Rechèrches sur les Porcelaines Chinoises* — Bulletin de la Société d'Encouragement pour l'Industrie Nationale, April 1900, pages 530—612

11 *L. N. Nikulina and T. I. Taraeva: *The Petrographic Features of Chinese Porcelain Stone* — Stecklo I Keramika 16 (8) 40—44 (1959)

12 Carl W. Correns: *Introduction to Mineralogy, Crystallography and Petrology* (Allen & Unwin, London, 1969; Heidelberg, New York)

13 A. D. Brankston: *Early Ming Wares of Ching-tê Chên* (Lund Humphries, 1970)

14   Margaret Medley: *The Chinese Potter* (Phaidon Press Ltd, 1976; Scribner, New York, 1976).

15   *P. C. Robinson: *Origin and Nature of Ceramic Fluxes* — Ceramics 16 (202) 34—37, 50 (1965)

16   Herbert H. Sanders: *The World of Japanese Ceramics* (Kodansha International, 1967)

17   Père d'Entrecolles: *Letters concerning the manufacture of Chinese porcelain written in Kiangsi in 1712 and 1722.* Translated by S. W. Bushell and reprinted in William Burton's book: *Porcelain, A Sketch of its Nature, Art and Manufacture* (Cassell, 1906, pages 84—122)

18   S. W. Bushell: *Oriental Ceramic Art* (New York 1899). Includes some partial translations of Chiang Ch'i's *Appendix on the Ceramic Industry* — pages 178—183

19   *Sundius, Dr Nils: *Some Aspects of the Technical Development in the Manufacture of the Chinese Pottery Wares of Pre-Ming Age* (Museum of Far Eastern Antiquities, Bulletin no. 33)

20   Ernst Rosenthal: *Pottery and Ceramics* (Penguin, 1949)

21   *Nigel Wood: *Chinese Porcelain* — Pottery Quarterly, Vol. 12, No. 47

22   Hermann Seger: *Collected Writings* (American Ceramics Society, 1902)

23   *Tsuneshi Ishii: *Experiments on the Kinuta Blue Celadon Glaze* — transactions of the British Ceramic Society, Wedgwood Bicentenary Memorial Number, 1930

24   *Tsuneshi Ishii: *Experiments on the Tenriuji Yellow Celadon Glaze* — same issue as above

25   *J. N. Collie: *Notes on some Chinese Glazes on Pottery and Porcelain* — transactions of the English Ceramic Society, 15, 160, 1915—16, pages 160—165

26   Walter Steger: *Porsilin* — publication of Gustavsberg Factory, Sweden, 3, 1951—52

27   Bernard Leach: *A Potter's Book* (Faber & Faber, 1945; Transatlantic Arts, New York, 1973)

28   A. L. Hetherington: *Chinese Ceramic Glazes* (Cambridge, 1937)

29   *W. H. Earhart: *Examination of a Chinese Temmoku Glaze and Body* — Bulletin of the American Ceramic Society, 20, (4), 121, 1941

30   *R. W. Jones: *Albany Slip Clay* — American Ceramic Society Transactions, Vol. 18 (1916) 242

31   *Richard P. Isaacs: *Albany Slip Clay* — American Ceramic Society Bulletin, August 1966, pages 714—715

32   *Bernard Moore and J. W. Mellor: *On the Manufacture of Felspathic or Hard Porcelain from British Raw Materials* — transactions of the British Ceramic Society, Wedgwood Bicentenary Memorial Number, 1930, pages 258—274

33   C. W. Parmelee: *Ceramic Glazes* (Chicago Industrial Publications, 1948)

34   *Paul E. Cox: *A Very White Glaze for Stoneware* — Ceramic Age,

Newark, Vol. 66, No. 3, September 1955, pages 41—42

35 *Ebelman and Salvetat: *Rechèrches sur la composition des matières employées dans la fabrication et dans la décoration de la porcelaine en Chine* — Annales de Chimie et Physique, 1851, pages 257—286

36 *J. S. Laird: *The Composition of Chinese Celadon Pottery* — Journal of the American Ceramic Society, 1, 1918, pages 675—678

37 H. Eccles and H. Rackham: *Analysed Specimens of English Porcelain* (Victoria and Albert Museum, 1922)

38 Joseph Grebanier: *Chinese Stoneware Glazes* (Pitman, London, 1975; Watson-Guptill, New York, 1975)

*Articles in journals

Index